C000199254

DIVE ISLE OF MAN

A DIVER GUIDE

Maura Mitchell and Ben Hextall

Underwater World Publications

Above: The shipbuilders' plate from the *Citrine* (site **9**)
Title page: Slipway at Peel

Maps drawn by Suzanne Hall

Designed and edited by Martyn Yeo

Produced by Diver Magazine

Published by Underwater World Publications Ltd,
55 High Street, Teddington, Middlesex, TW11 8HA

ISBN 0 946020 21 3

Printed in the United Arab Emirates by Emirates Printing Press,
PO Box 5106, Airport Road, Dubai

FOREWORD

by the Chief Executive of the Isle of Man
Department of Tourism

Enjoyed by people world-wide, sub aqua diving is a very popular sport. Divers are always seeking new places to explore underwater and I am sure they will be delighted with what the Isle of Man has to offer.

We have no less than seven diving clubs plus a dive school in a total population equal to that of a small English town – surely an indication of the quality of the diving!

Popular for holidays since Victorian times, with such a variety of things to do and see, the Isle of Man makes an excellent choice for the diver with a family, unlike some more remote destinations.

This guide fulfils a long overdue need for comprehensive information on how to succeed in getting the best dives. Where to launch, where to obtain air, the tides, weather and wrecks are all fully covered by the authors.

Why not come to dive the Isle of Man and enjoy all that this unique, friendly place has to offer? I am sure you will not regret it!

Terry Toohey
Chief Executive
Department of Tourism

Black sea cucumber (*Aslia lefevrei*) with its feeding tentacles

CONTENTS

HOW TO USE THIS GUIDE

This dive guide for the Isle of Man is intended to be utilised by local and visiting divers, as the island offers such excellent and rewarding dives. It roughly adheres to the format used for the other titles in the Dive Guide series, ensuring that the information is concise and "diver friendly".

As well as the maps and charts described below and the publications produced by the Tourist Board, there is a wealth of books on all manner of subjects relating to the Isle of Man, including many for children. Good bookshops will be found in all the main towns on the island. A list of books on marine life is given on page 28.

Hotels and Commissioners' offices always keep leaflets of forthcoming events and activities. The local newspapers and the telephone directory are also valuable sources of information. Several useful telephone numbers are listed on page 5.

Map references

All grid references are to the Ordnance Survey map of the Isle of Man (Sheet 95, scale 1:50,000) and are expressed in this style: SC 242 845. All Decca readings are given in degrees, minutes and hundredths of minutes, north and west, for example: 54 07 06N; 004 53 39W.

The *Isle of Man Public Rights of Way and Outdoor Leisure Map* is very informative (scale 1:25,000). In its fifth edition at the time of writing, it is published by the Department of the Environment at £4 and is by far the best map available. It is obtainable at most newsagents and bookshops on the island. The Isle of Man Tourist Board also produce a map that provides further local information, including street plans for the towns, slipways, moorings and even shipwrecks!

The Admiralty Charts are also invaluable. Chart No. 2094 covers the area from just south of the Isle of Man to the Mull of Galloway while Chart No. 2696 covers Douglas Bay and includes the main harbours on the Isle of Man.

Opposite: Maughold Head and the lighthouse

Dive sites and the standard dive sheet

The coastline around the Isle of Man has been divided into six areas as follows. Individual dive sites within these areas are listed in numerical order in the contents list and in alphabetical order in the index:

THE SOUTH-WEST – Contrary Head to the Calf Sound (sites **1** to **21**)

THE CALF OF MAN (sites **22** to **35**)

THE SOUTH – Spanish Head to Fort Island (sites **36** to **60**)

THE SOUTH-EAST – Derbyhaven to Douglas Head (sites **61** to **72**)

THE NORTH-EAST – Douglas Bay to the Point of Ayre (sites **73** to **88**)

THE NORTH-WEST – Point of Ayre to Contrary Head (sites **89** and **90**)

There is a dive sheet for each dive, which follows a standard layout intended to provide all the necessary information in an easy-to-follow and concise format. The format of the dive sheets is shown on page 33 and each sheet should be read in conjunction with the accompanying site map.

A blank dive sheet is printed on page 140. Information regarding additional dive sites worthy of revisiting may be filled in. Also, it is inevitable that some information may become outdated or perhaps a new shipwreck is discovered!

The authors would be most grateful for information regarding any new dive sites, as well as amendments. Please send these to Maura Mitchell and Ben Hextall, c/o Underwater World Publications Ltd, 55 High Street, Teddington, Middlesex, TW11 8HA.

Opposite: The six areas covered by this guide

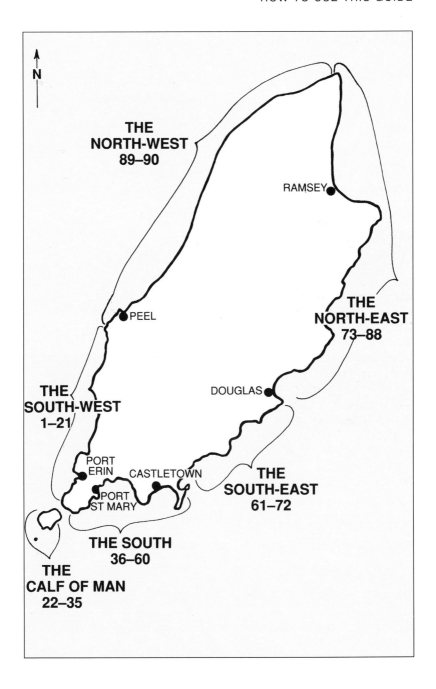

Laxey – inner harbour and slipway

Nemertisia antennina is common in the fast-flowing currents

4

USEFUL TELEPHONE NUMBERS

Please note that the new British Telecom dialling codes have been used throughout this guide. Although their use was optional when the text was being prepared, they must be used from 16 April 1995.

Isle of Man Tourist Board: 01624 686766 or 01624 686868 (24-hour brochure request line)

Ronaldsway Airport – general enquiries: 01624 823311

Manx Airlines: 01624 824313

Isle of Man Steam Packet Company: 01624 661661

Noble's Hospital: 01624 663322

Chandlers – Manx Marine Ltd, 35 North Quay, Douglas: 01624 674842

Outboard engine repairs and maintenance – Ballasalla Marine and Auto Engineers, Balathane Industrial Estate, Ballasalla: 01624 822715

Diving school – Southern Diving Lodge: 01624 832943

ABOUT THE ISLE OF MAN

The Isle of Man has been a popular holiday destination since Victorian times, and this section provides the visiting diver – together with family or groups – the information needed for enjoyment and entertainment.

Travel

The Isle of Man is very easy to get to from England, Scotland, Wales and Ireland. There are frequent flights from all major UK airports through Manx Airlines. The Isle of Man Steam Packet Company operates ferry services to Douglas from Heysham, Liverpool, Belfast and Dublin.

The Isle of Man Tourist Board can provide all tourist information, including accommodation, travel and events throughout the year (such as TT Week).

Places to visit

The following information is just a brief description of some of the numerous sites and activities on the Isle of Man. For more detailed information contact the Tourist Board.

Port Erin   Port Erin is a popular holiday destination, with a large, safe, sandy beach. There is plenty to see and do: the Railway Museum, Bradda Glen and the Marine Interpretation Centre at the Marine Laboratory.

The Calf of Man   The Calf of Man is a 616-acre islet separated from the main Isle of Man by the waters of the Sound. The wild and rocky islet is preserved by the Manx National Trust and is home to part of its flock of the native Manx sheep, the Loghtan. It is a sanctuary for birds and forms part of a chain of observatories throughout the British Isles. In summer and subject to the weather, boat trips to and around the Calf are available from Port Erin and Port St Mary.

Opposite: Nesting kittewakes

Cregneash   Cregneash Village Folk Museum is a unique illustration of 19th-century life in a Manx upland crofting community. Traditional crafts are demonstrated weekly throughout the summer.

Port St Mary   Port St Mary is a busy fishing village, with pleasant beaches and walks around the harbour.

Castletown   Castle Rushen, at the heart of the island's ancient capital, Castletown, is one of Britain's most complete medieval castles. The Castle has its origins in the Norse period and the last Viking king, Magnus, died here in 1265. The settlement that grew up here to serve the castle became the main government centre and the island's capital until the major port of Douglas took over in 1869. Castle Rushen houses some spectacular recreated displays of life in the medieval and 17th-century periods.

The Nautical Museum, situated at the mouth of the harbour, contains an 18th-century armed yacht, *The Peggy*, built in 1791. This vessel is shown in her original boathouse where she remained undisturbed for a century after her owner's death, being rediscovered in 1935. A replica sailmaker's loft, ship models, other exhibits and photographs bring alive the Manx maritime life and trade in the days of sail.

The Old Grammar School was built around 1200 as the capital's first church. St Mary's Chapel also played an important role in the history of Manx education.

The Derby Fort on Fort Island was built around 1560 as part of Henry VIII's scheme of coastal defences and was restored a hundred years later, in order to withstand the forces of the Parliament at the time of the English Civil War.

Douglas   Start your discovery of Manx national heritage at the Manx Museum, where a specially produced film portrayal of Manx history introduces the visitor to the unique Story of Mann. The visitor can proceed through a sequence of newly designed galleries depicting art, historic maps, natural history, prehistoric, Viking and early medieval archaeology, and social history. New galleries show tourism, TT and the finance sector.

Laxey   A former mining village built in a deep valley. This very pretty village is kept neat and tidy, and houses the great Laxey Wheel, Lady Isabella, built in 1854 to pump water from the mines of the Great Laxey Mining Company. This masterpiece of 19th-century engineering has a diameter of 22 metres and remains the largest working waterwheel in the world. The Laxey woollen mills are well worth a visit for hand-woven tweeds and the Electric Tramway has a branch line running from here to the top of Snaefell.

Ramsey   The Grove Rural Life Museum is a time-capsule Victorian period house on the outskirts of Ramsey. The outbuildings contain an interesting collection of vehicles and agricultural implements.

Mooragh Park on the north side of Ramsey has a large boating lake bordered by sheltered gardens and palm trees. Its café is open in summer. Curraghs Wildlife Park has a collection of animals from around the world displayed in large paddocks on a geographical basis. A nature trail into the Curraghs wetlands provides a link to Manx wildlife.

The North-West   The Point of Ayre is at the northern tip of the Isle of Man, with a prominent lighthouse. The land is fairly flat, with the exception of the Bride Hills. The north-west coast is a wild, unspoilt, 12-mile curve of sand, shingle and cobble beaches, with dunes and sandy cliffs. The Ayres, a Manx National Trust nature reserve, is home to nesting terns and other wildlife. A smaller reserve, Cronk y Bing, lies further down the coast. The Raad ny Foillan coastal footpath hugs the edge of the beach. Further south the footpath goes inland, around Kirk Michael, then back along the sandstone cliffs of Gob ny Creggan, past caves at Gob y Deigan, Wills Strand and along to Peel Bay.

Raad ny Foillan   This coastal footpath, signposted with a blue sign depicting a gull in flight, is about 90 miles long and follows the coastline

Break between dives at Cabby Ghaw, Calf Sound

around the Isle of Man, from the flat shingle beaches of the north to the steep cliffs of the south. There are two other long walks on the island: the Bayr ny Skeddan from Peel to Castletown and the Millennium Way from Ramsey to Castletown.

Peel   Peel Castle, one of the Isle of Man's principal historic monuments, occupies the important site of St Patrick's Isle. In the 11th century the castle became the ruling seat of the Norse kingdom of Mann and the Isles.

Odin's Raven is a two-thirds size replica of the famous Gokstad ship excavated from the Viking burial near Oslo. It was sailed 1500 miles across the North Sea to Peel in 1979 by a crew of 16 Manxmen and Norwegians in an epic voyage celebrating the millennium of Tynwald, the island's parliament. The story of this voyage is presented in the boathouse, which contains this beautifully built boat.

The stepped Tynwald Hill at St Johns is a reminder of the 1000-year-old origins of Tynwald, the Manx parliament. The Tynwald craft centre and woollen mills are well worth a visit.

Geology

Although some people shy away from the word "geology", a basic knowledge gives an understanding and insight to the very "bones" of the places we visit and dive. In the main, the Isle of Man consists of Manx slate series that can be seen everywhere: the material of miles of roadside walls, gateposts and pillars, churches and cottages. Large slabs form steps and lintels over doors and windows.

Beyond the hills and mountains, the flat plains of the north start with the raised beaches of wind blown sand. Red marls and sandstone form the rolling hills of Bride. Reaching across from Andreas to Jurby Head is an underlying band of carboniferous limestone, with a further band of basement conglomerates just north of Ramsey. West of Ramsey, through the Curraghs to Ballough, lies an alluvium plain. The coast north of Peel also consists of basement conglomerates. Peel Castle is built mainly of sandstone, which, although easily worked, erodes rapidly with time.

The area in the south, bounded by Poyll Vaaish, Colby, Ballasalla, Cass-ny-Hawin and Castletown, consists mainly of carboniferous limestone. The well preserved Castle Rushen is constructed of this hard material, as are many of the surrounding buildings. The exposed carboniferous volcanic rocks on the coast between Scarlett and Poyll Vaaish, a distance of just over a mile, possess more attractions for the geologist than any other portion of the island. The visitors' centre at

Burroo Rock, with its distinctive "eye". There are a number of different routes to take on this excellent site (site **32**)

Scarlett can provide information on geology. The interesting arches found along the Castletown Bay side of Langness are formed from carboniferous basement conglomerate over red stained Manx slates.

Viewed from the sea, the cliffs of Marine Drive have, in places, very noticeable contorted folding of the bedded slates. The north-west face of Bradda Head also has spectacular folding, with intrusion veins of white quartz and patches of rust-coloured hematite (iron ore). Further north, towards the wreck of the *Citrine*, are the remains of old mine buildings, and quartz outcrops bear green stains indicating the presence of copper ore. Extensive mining was undertaken here in the past and as a consequence the whole headland is riddled with mine workings – for safety these are all blocked off.

The sea cliffs from Peel southwards and up the east coast to Ramsey are a haven for sea birds. Horizontal ledges formed in the weathered slates make perfect nesting sites for guillemots and razorbills. Terns nest among the dunes and scrub at the Ayres. Underwater, the slates form more ledges and caves, pinnacles and stacks, providing a multitude of habitats for every kind of marine creature.

DIVING

The Isle of Man offers some of the most spectacular and varied diving in the British Isles. The coastline is unspoilt and the water relatively unpolluted. The marine life is highly diverse, the underwater visibility generally superb and the dive sites unspoilt.

Harbours and launch sites

All the main towns have excellent launching slips that can be used at most states of the tide.

Port Erin Port Erin, with its deep, sheltered bay open only to the north-west, is without doubt the best known and favourite place for divers. A slipway on the south side of the bay near Raglan Pier leads to the firm, sandy beach. Boats may be moored next to Raglan Pier (near which are toilets and fresh water) and a little further on is a jetty that is ideal for loading and unloading kit and divers. There are also two mooring buoys for visiting boats, located 50 metres north of the jetty.

When night diving from a boat, note that the large green conical buoy marking the end of the breakwater is unfortunately not illuminated. Instead, a safe course may be made by placing the lighthouse at the northern end of Port Erin beach directly underneath the red leading light on the promenade above. There is also a lighthouse on the end of Raglan Pier opposite the Harbour Master's office (tel. 01624 833205).

Port St Mary Port St Mary has an excellent harbour and the large pier provides a good, sheltered launch site. The wide public slipway is just inside the pier and is usable at all states of the tide. Access to this slipway must not be blocked as it is used by the inshore lifeboat. Just above this slipway are toilets and a fresh water supply, and ample parking space. The Harbour Master's office is situated next to the inner harbour (tel. 01624 833206).

Opposite: Diver on the boiler of the *Mayfield* (site **1**)

13

Port Erin harbour

Castletown   The outer harbour is quite sheltered from all but easterly winds but, unfortunately, is dry for much of the tide. The wide slipway is usable only for about two hours around high water. Parking is limited on the quayside, but there is a car park behind the harbour that provides plenty of space. Parking disks are needed, obtainable from the Town Hall (near Castletown Square) or from any Post Office. Harbour Master: tel. 01624 823549.

Castletown Promenade Slipway   On the road leading from Castletown to Derbyhaven is a fairly steep concrete slipway leading to an excellent beach of firm sand. Launching is good, except towards low water when areas of boulders and weed are a problem. Parking is available on the road.

Derbyhaven   Mud abounds! Launching and successful recovery is best achieved two hours either side of high water – or else you need a good four-wheel-drive vehicle! The pebble beach runs onto soft sand and clay. Very sheltered – only exposed to north-easterly winds.

Douglas   There is an excellent public slipway on the South Quay, located near the lifeboat house and almost opposite Diving Air Services. The slipway is usable at all states of the tide, though care must be taken at low water on spring tides. Toilets may be found at the end of the South Quay, near the gas depot. There is a limited amount of parking.

Diving is not permitted in or around this busy commercial harbour. The new breakwater, constructed from triangular interlocking stabit blocks, may appear to be a good dive site, but again it is not permitted – wave surge can also trap divers between the blocks. The slipway is used for most boat diving in the south-east and north-east areas. Harbour Control, day or night: tel. 01624 686628.

Laxey   Very sheltered inner harbour with a good, wide slipway that is usable about two hours either side of high water. With a good four-wheel-drive vehicle it is possible to launch over firm ground up to the harbour entrance. There is plenty of free parking by the harbour, in front of Laxey Pipes. Toilets are situated by the Harbour Control on the quay. Harbour Control: tel. 01624 861663.

Ramsey   There are two slipways for public use. The first is opposite the lifeboat house near the harbour entrance. This slipway leads to firm sand and is usable at all states of the tide, although a four-wheel-drive vehicle is recommended. Care should be taken when launching and recovering at low water in the vicinity of the harbour wall, as the sand there tends to be unstable. Do not block lifeboat access on the slipway. Toilets are located behind the swimming pool.

The slipway at Port St Mary

The other public slipway is situated on the north side of the inner harbour but is only usable two hours either side of high water. Harbour Control, East Quay: tel. 01624 812245.

Peel   The sheltered public slipway is located near the castle, next to the outer breakwater. It has been extensively modified and is usable at all states of the tide. To reach it, go over the bridge at the top of the harbour and drive along the west side towards the castle. There is limited parking space, and special attention must be taken not to block lifeboat access. There are toilets near the slipway and during the summer snacks and ices are available from a kiosk.

Tides and weather

A large tidal range (over 8 metres on spring tides) means that exceptionally strong currents are common around the island. Some sites should therefore only be attempted on neap tides or slack water. Unfortunately, these rarely coincide with high or low water!

Inshore currents by headlands and in certain areas are very strong and do not always run in the same direction as offshore tidal streams marked on charts. Bays often have contra-rotating currents. The areas around the Calf Sound, Chicken Rock, the Burroo, Stack, the south tip of Langness and the Point of Ayre have overfalls, standing waves and very fast rip currents. Divers should only dive at these sites with knowledge of the slack water times. If in doubt, consult local divers.

The times of high and low water in the Isle of Man are approximately the same as those predicted for Liverpool ($\pm$ 5 minutes), but the tidal range is approximately 3 metres smaller. *Laver's Liverpool and Irish Sea Tide Table* is available from newsagents, dive shops and yacht chandlers or direct from Laver publishing, PO Box 7, Liverpool L19 9EN (tel. 0151-709 1465). Maps showing the tides around the Isle of Man appear on pages 17–21.

The Manx Sailing and Cruising Club has produced a book of tidal streams. This is available from the Club at North Quay, Ramsey (tel. 01624 813494) or from the Bridge Book Shop, Shore Road, Port Erin (tel. 01624 833376).

Tide times for the Calf of Man are shown on the map on page 61. The times given are for spring tides; a little more time allowance can be given for neap tides.

The average water temperature ranges from 6°C in February/March to 14°C in August/September.

Underwater visibility tends to be very good, reaching 15 to 20 metres during the summer and early autumn. It averages 5 metres in the winter, occasionally less after storms or during the plankton blooms (the main plankton bloom occurs during May). Due to the strong currents, visibility improves very rapidly after storms, clearing in 24 to 48 hours.

The prevailing wind is westerly to south-westerly.

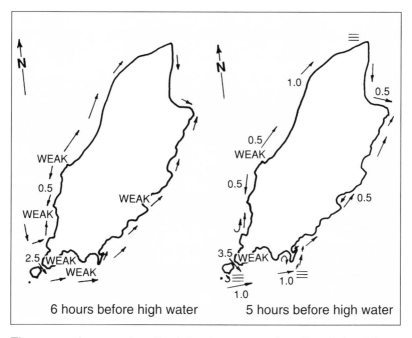

6 hours before high water   5 hours before high water

The maps above and on the following pages show the state of the tides at hourly intervals either side of high water

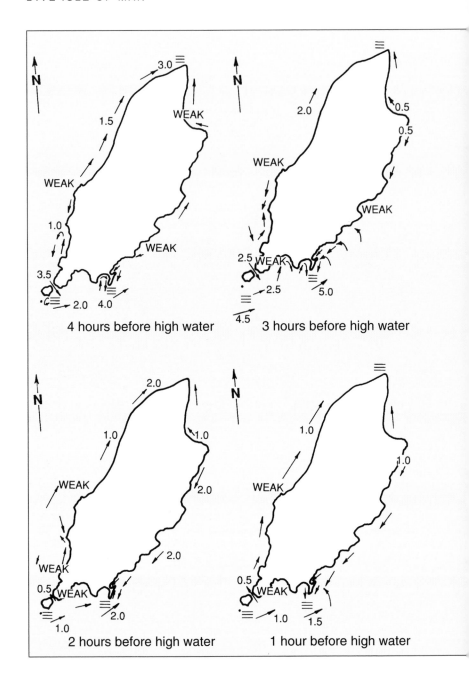

4 hours before high water

3 hours before high water

2 hours before high water

1 hour before high water

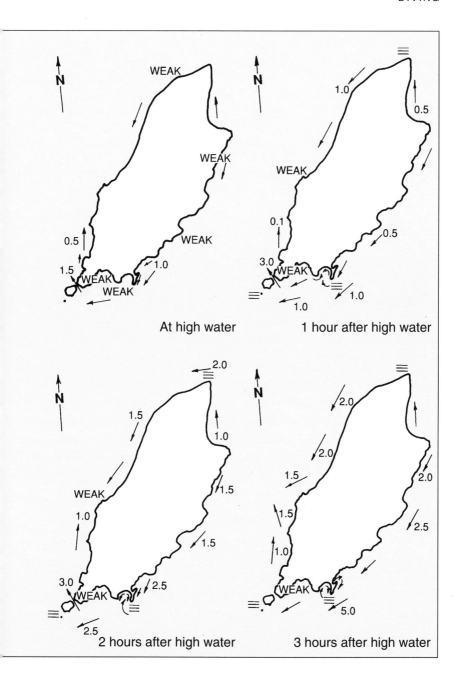

At high water

1 hour after high water

2 hours after high water

3 hours after high water

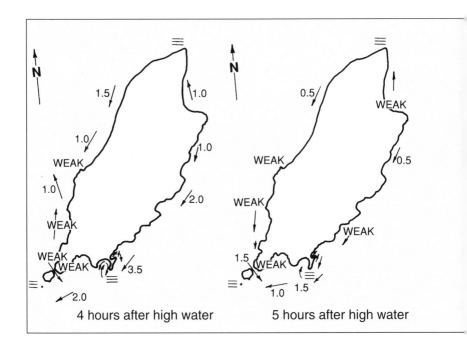

4 hours after high water   5 hours after high water

Air

Air can be obtained from:

Aquatech, 10 Hudson's Yard, Lime Street, Port St Mary (between the Harbour Master's office and the lifeboat station). Specialist diving services (full service facility) including mixed gas, hydro testing and regulator servicing. Open long hours, including weekends, by demand during the dive season. Tel. 01624 833037.

Diving Air Services, South Quay, Douglas. Open Monday to Friday, 0900 to 1730 and Saturday 0900 to 1300. Closed Thursday afternoons. Tel. 01624 628123.

Hyperbaric Centre, The Fire Station, Peel Road, Douglas. Open Monday to Friday, 0900 to 1700. Tel. 01624 626394. Also able to fill oxygen cylinders. See page 30.

Wrecks

There are many wrecks lying in the waters around the Isle of Man. In the past, the majority were small timber vessels: fishing smacks, cutters,

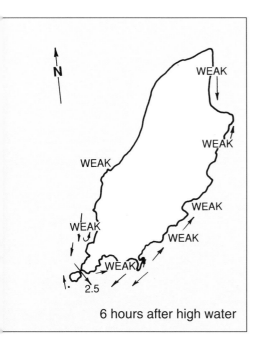

WEAK

WEAK

WEAK

WEAK

WEAK

WEAK

WEAK

2.5

6 hours after high water

sloops and merchant schooners. Over the years hundreds of ships have perished, soon to be reduced to matchwood – any floating pieces were eagerly collected for building. Steel vessels that were wrecked on the coast soon succumbed to winter gales and ended up as mere skeletons with projecting ribs and scattered plates.

Offshore, in deeper water, many wrecks have survived more or less intact, but are slowly sinking into the sea bed. The main cause is the tidal currents flowing across the wreckage, forming scour pits and accelerating the sinking.

The wreck laws – the Wreck and Salvage (Ships and Aircraft) Act 1979 and the Protection of Wrecks (Designation) Order 1982 – apply to all wrecks, so nothing should be removed from them. Many wrecks are the property of local people or sub-aqua clubs and should not be dived without permission.

The Isle of Man Sub-Aqua Club owns the wreck of HMS *Racehorse*, located on the Skerranes rocks, Langness. There is a large exclusion area around this wreck of historic interest – specifically "an area 350 metres radius around a position 54 3 12N; 004 37 73W, but excluding any part which falls above the high water mark of ordinary spring tides" – and it should not be dived without permission. See notes on pages 93–4.

A group of students at the Marine Station own the *Our Lassie* and regulate diving on the *Don Bosco*. Anyone wishing to dive these wrecks should get in touch with the Diving Officer of the Port Erin Marine Biologists' Sub-Aqua Club (tel. 01624 832027).

For more information on Isle of Man shipwrecks telephone John Kermode on 01624 851947.

Fishing regulations

The Isle of Man has a 12-mile fishery protection limit. A £500 fine can and has been imposed for contravening any of the following regulations:

Scallops: Out of season 31 May to 1 November. Minimum size 11 cm.

Crabs: Minimum size 11.5 cm. Must not be taken berried or soft.

Lobsters: Minimum size 23 cm. Must not be taken berried or soft.

Spearfishing is totally banned.

Marine life

There is a wonderfully diverse range of marine life in the waters around the Isle of Man. Marine animals and plants feature in this book, and in order to keep the dive sheets as simple as possible, common names are used wherever possible.

One commonly term used is "kelp forest community". This refers collectively to all the animals and plants associated with kelp, such as encrusting red algae, sponges, mobile crustaceans and fish.

The following list of scientific names has been collated using common names from the *Field Guide to the Water Life of Britain*. It is by no means complete, but it does provide an insight into the vast amount of marine life around the Isle of Man.

Algae
Eel grass – *Zostera marina*
Forest kelp – *Laminaria hyperborea*
Bootlace weed – *Chorda filum*
Sugar kelp – *Laminaria saccharina*
Oarweed – *Laminaria digitata*
Furbelows – *Sacchoriza polyschides*
Dabberlocks – *Alaria esculenta*

Tubularia indivisia – oaten pipes hydroid

Sponges
Elephant's ear sponge – *Pachymatisma johnstonia*
Boring sponge – *Cliona celata*
Breadcrumb sponge – *Halichondria panicea*

Hydroids (sea firs)
Oaten pipes hydroid – *Tubularia indivisa*
Nemertesia antennina

Sea anemones (anthozoa)
Burrowing or tube anemone – *Cerianthus lloydii*
Beadlet anemone – *Actinia equina*
Snakelocks anemone – *Anemonia sulcata*
Plumose anemone – *Metridium senile*
Dahlia anemone – *Urticina felina*
Actinothoë sphyrodeta
Jewel anemone – *Corynactis viridis*
Devonshire cup coral – *Caryophyllia smithii*
Dead man's fingers – *Alcyonium digitatum*

Henricia sanguinolenta – bloody Henry

Botryllus schlosseri – star sea squirt

Segmented worms (annelidia)
Peacock worm – *Sabella pavonina*
Feather duster worm – *Bispira volutacornis*
Sand mason worm – *Lanice conchilega*

Molluscs
Edible cockle – *Cerastoderma edule*
Common mussel – *Mytilus edulis*
Sea slug (nudibranch)- *Facelina auriculata*
Sea lemon (nudibranch)- *Archidoris pseudoargus*
Sea hare – *Aplysia punctata*
Great scallop – *Pecten maximus*
Common cuttlefish – *Sepia officinalis*
Lesser octopus – *Eledone cirrhosa*

Crustaceans
Aesop prawn – *Pandalus montagui*
Common shrimp – *Crangon crangon*
Common lobster – *Homarus gammarus*
Spiny squat lobster – *Galathea strigosa*
Hermit crab – *Pagurus bernhardus*
Edible crab – *Cancer pagurus*
Velvet crab – *Liocarcinus puber*

Bryozoans
Hairy sea mat – *Electra pilosa*
Ross coral or rose coral – *Pentapora foliacea*
Hornwrack – *Flustra foliacea*

Echinoderms
Featherstar – *Antedon bifida*
Bloody Henry – *Henricia* spp.
Common sunstar – *Crossaster papposus*
Common starfish – *Asterias rubens*
Common brittlestar – *Ophiothrix fragilis*
Spiny starfish – *Marthasterias glacialis*
Common or edible sea urchin – *Echinus esculentus*

Sea squirts
Gooseberry sea squirt – *Dendrodoa grossularia*
Star sea squirt – *Botryllus schlosseri*
Morchellium argus
Aplidium spp.

Fish
Lesser spotted dogfish – *Scyliorhinus canicula*
Conger eel – *Conger conger*
Sand eel – *Ammonites tobianus*
Bib – *Trisopterus luscus*
Whiting – *Merlangius merlangus*
Pollack – *Pollachius pollachius*
Saithe or coley – *Pollachius virens*
Common ling – *Molva molva*
Greater pipefish – *Syngnathus acus*
Cuckoo wrasse – *Labrus mixtus*
Ballan wrasse – *Labrus bergylta*
Corkwing wrasse – *Crenilabrus melops*
Butterfish – *Pholis gunnellus*
Blenny – *Blennius* spp.
Plaice – *Pleuronectes platessa*
Topknot – *Zeugopterus punctatus*
Two-spotted goby – *Gobiusculus flavescens*
Sea scorpion – *Taurulus bubalis*

Basking sharks   From mid summer onwards, divers may be fortunate enough to observe basking sharks feeding on zooplankton around the west and south coast of the Isle of Man. These huge, harmless filter feeders have been coming for many years, though they have been observed in large numbers only since 1988.

The Marine Conservation Society initiated a Shark Watch programme for the British Isles in the early 1980s. This also proved a great success in Manx waters, thanks to the considerable numbers of sharks and to the assistance of Marine Conservation Society members, Port Erin Marine Laboratory, boat owners, the Isle of Man Steam Packet Company and other members of the public. Valuable local information obtained about the sharks generated considerable interest around the world. Ken Watterson now organises the Isle of Man Basking Shark Project and would be pleased to have records of numbers, size, activity and location of any sharks – call the Shark Watch line on 01624 801207. Forms for recording sightings are available; sightings of whales and dolphins should also be reported.

If you see any of these marine creatures, please do not chase them or drive your boat directly towards them. Switch off the engine and drift with them – they will often approach you. Refrain from making a noise, splashing or leaping in or they will submerge.

Conger eel (*Conger conger*) with "housekeeping" prawns (*Pandalus montagui*)

Colourful scorpion fish – *Taurulus bubalis*

Ballan wrasse are very tame

Further reading   The following publications are highly recommended for divers more interested in marine life:
The Marine Conservation Society Guide to Inshore Marine Life, David Erwin and Bernard Picton, Immel Publishing, London, 1987.
Collins Pocket Guide to the Sea Shore, John H. Barrett and C.M. Yonge, Collins, London, 1958.
Field Guide to the Water Life of Britain, Reader's Digest Association, London, 1984.
Marine Fauna of the Isle of Man, edited by J.R. Bruce, J.S. Colman and N.S. Jones, Liverpool University Press, Second Edition, 1963. This very comprehensive reference book is available cheaply, while stocks last, through Port Erin Marine Laboratory (tel. 01624 832027).

Conservation

Conservation of the underwater environment is of increasing importance to the diver. It is hoped that no local or visiting divers will in any way contravene the fishery regulations of the Isle of Man (see page 22).

Intensive potting of crabs and lobsters, along with dredging for scallops over many years has decimated stocks, so the taking of shellfish by divers must be self-regulating, with a voluntary code of practice to avoid the risk of any future legislation.

While underwater, please avoid damaging delicate marine life by good buoyancy practice and careful finning. Divers must at all times adhere to the BSAC code of conduct (see Appendix 2) and follow safe diving practices.

Diving safety

Safety at sea   The Coastguard is based in Liverpool (tel. 0151-931 3341 or 0151-931 3343). In an emergency dial 999 and ask for the Coastguard. Alternatively the Coastguard can be reached using a VHF radio and calling on Channel 16.

The weather on the Isle of Man is very changeable. All dive boats should be adequately equipped, and should carry flares, a radio, an anchor with sufficient line and life-jackets.

Ronaldsway Meteorological Office provides a shipping forecast (tel. 01696 888322) and a weather check (tel. 01696 888300 or if off the island 01696 888200). At the time of writing calls are charged at 30p per minute and the service is updated at approximately 0730, 1200 and 1800 each day. MetFax provides dial-up forecasts and weather information (tel. 01336 400401 for the index page). Local Manx Radio (1368 MHz) provides weather information following the news, with regular updates.

On the fishing boat *Don Bosco* (site **4**)

Hyperbaric Centre The Hyperbaric Centre is regarded as one of the best in Europe. It is situated behind Douglas Fire Station on Peel Road and has all the appearances of a modern medical centre. It was opened in 1992 to replace the facility established in 1987 in memory of local commercial diver Kevin Grey. It is administered by the Kevin Grey Memorial Trust and has more than proved the need for hyperbaric treatment as a valuable addition to the community medical services. The opening formalities were performed jointly by Mr W. Scholl of the Dr Scholl Foundation who funded the Hyperbaric Centre building and Dr Henry B. Dyer for the Pacini Charitable Foundation, which funded the majority of the equipment including the large medical chamber.

There are currently two chambers in operation. The smaller chamber (4.5 x 2.2 metres) is primarily kept available for diving emergencies. The larger chamber (6.5 x 2.8 metres) is mainly used for medical treatment but also has full operating theatre capabilities. Both chambers are of twin lock construction, 5 bar rated and fully equipped for the management of the unconscious patient. The whole complex is run by a highly qualified technical operator and nurse and two hyperbarically qualified doctors are available to advise on treatment on 24-hour call. Up to 150 medical treatments are undertaken every week via referrals from specialists and doctors. The majority of these are hyperbaric oxygen therapy for non-diving related problems, but the chamber has been used on several occasions to treat decompression sickness.

Oxygen is manufactured on site and during working hours diving cylinders and oxygen cylinders can be filled. All charges go towards the running costs of the facility.

To arrange group visits or obtain advice on other matters telephone the Hyperbaric Centre on 01624 626394.

DIVING EMERGENCIES

In the event of a diving emergency, a 999 call asking for the Coastguard must be made. Alternatively call on Channel 16 using a VHF radio.
The Coastguard will then take control of the situation.

Decompression sickness Any trained diver should be able immediately to recognise the symptoms of decompression sickness or the "bends" and the procedure to be followed is described later in this section.

It is most important not to ignore any untoward symptoms after diving. Failure to take symptoms seriously could wreck a life or even lose it – do not hesitate to seek help. Decompression sickness is far more likely to occur in the diver on holiday for several reasons:

Repeat diving The diver on holiday naturally tries to pack in as much as possible! Spread your dives sensibly over the day, giving as much surface interval as possible. Relax between dives.

Deep diving Planning (and sticking to the plan), preparation and work-up dives of increasing depth are all part of safe diving. Diving computers are now so widely used that few divers take the trouble to pre-calculate bottom times. "Diving to the line" with a computer seems to be very prevalent. But remember that a dive computer is not a magic charm! Do your deepest dive first.

Dehydration Dehydration lowers blood volume and is one of the causes of unexpected decompression sickness. Full blood volume is necessary to get rid of excess nitrogen when decompressing. Drink plenty of fluid before, between and after dives – water, fruit juice, or hot drinks if chilly are preferable to coffee (a diuretic), alcohol or fizzy drinks.

Exercise It is not good to undertake heavy exercise before or after diving as this too can cause dehydration and depletion of blood volume.

Alcohol If you go in for heavy drinking, wait until the end of your holiday. A diver with a hangover is not the safest buddy.

Altitude Keep in mind the possible dangers of travelling up into the hills immediately after a dive. Even after a single dive, well within the tables, extra gassing off of nitrogen whilst gaining altitude can cause problems. Like flying after diving, it is not recommended.

Opposite: Inner harbour, Port St Mary

Take a break   A build-up of nitrogen occurs after several days of consecutive diving. Take a break to allow nitrogen levels to return to normal. There is certainly no lack of things to do and see on your day off in the Isle of Man!

Decompression accidents   The procedure to be followed is laid down in the *Safe Diving Practices* leaflet compiled by the National Diving Committee of the British Sub-Aqua Club. This says:

"Decompression sickness symptoms vary between those so sudden that immediate air evacuation to a chamber is vital, to those which may not become apparent for some hours. Some of these less dramatic symptoms, which may well be delayed, can be more serious and produce greater disability than the excruciating pain associated with a joint bend. Tingling and numbness are included in this category.

"Air embolism or severe decompression sickness symptoms occurring at sea require rapid transfer of the subject to a recompression chamber, laid flat on their back and, if possible, the administration of 100% oxygen. Being bounced rapidly in a small boat is almost certainly going to worsen the symptoms rather than help the situation. RAF search and rescue helicopters will almost certainly be involved in the above situation the use of VHF radio is essential. HM Coastguard, although co-ordinating all rescues at sea, are not medically qualified to diagnose diving related medical disorders and have to seek advice before activating a Medivac air evacuation.

"The Department of Transport and British Telecom International (BTI) operate a radio medical advisory service through the BTI coast radio stations. If your radio has a Duplex operating system with coast radio station working frequencies it is advisable to contact the nearest coast radio station where you will be put in direct contact with a doctor via a telephone link. There is no charge for this service. If your radio does not have coast radio station frequencies or has a Simplex operating system it is advisable to contact the Coastguard on Channel 16. This may take more time, as the Coastguard will have to contact the doctor on your behalf. If the situation is serious enough a PAN PAN call would be necessary.

"If decompression sickness symptoms arise on land and they are serious, you are advised to dial 999 and ask for an ambulance, explaining the symptoms on the phone. If a helicopter is needed, the doctor will contact the Coastguard (if you are on the coast), who will co-ordinate the rescue. Inland, rapid transport with police escort can be arranged by the medical emergency services."

Dive number and name of dive site

Position Grid reference for inshore sites, latitude and longitude for offshore sites.

Type of Dive Whether the dive is a scenic, wreck or drift dive.

Level of Dive The level the authors consider appropriate. The dive marshal or diving officer will be able to ascertain personal ability and suitability. Four qualification grades are given to describe the experience level required: novice diver, sports diver, dive leader and advanced diver. Inclement site conditions will obviously alter the experience level required.

Access Shore or boat dive (for the latter the most suitable launch site is also given).

Max Depth Usually at high water.

DESCRIPTION: A brief description of the dive site, how the wreck happened, where the cliff leads to, and how to get the best out of the dive.

WHAT TO LOOK FOR: Marine life, wreckage, gullies.

OTHER INFORMATION: Tidal information and other hazards, such as nets.

Standard dive sheet layout

ROCKS BETWEEN HIGH WATER AND LOW WATER		■ BUILDING
SAND		**86** DIVE SITE NUMBER
CLIFF		— ·— UNDERSEA CABLE
UNDERWATER FEATURE		→1.0 DIRECTION OF CURRENT AND SPEED IN KNOTS
WRECK		≡ OVERFALLS AND STANDING WAVES
←- -→ SUGGESTED DIVE ROUTE (SEE TEXT)		WEAK TIDE ABOUT TO TURN

Key to the symbols used on the dive site maps

THE SOUTH-WEST

This area covers dive sites from Peel to the south-west tip of the island, including Port Erin. Apart from the wreck of the *Mayfield* and Niarbyl, the area between Contrary Head and Fleshwick tends to be shallow and sandy, and the dives are less interesting than those further south. However, this area is so little dived that it could be well worth exploring. There are many little bays, beaches and rocky headlands between Contrary Head and Niarbyl, which are all interesting dives, though quite similar. This stretch of coast is inaccessible by road, but can be traversed by the Raad ny Foillan coastal footpath from Peel to Glen Maye. The views and wildlife along this section of the footpath are spectacular.

1 Mayfield

Position – SC 211 784. *Type of Dive* – Wreck. *Level of Dive* – Novice Diver. *Access* – Boat Dive (launch Port Erin or Peel). *Max Depth* – 16m.

DESCRIPTION: Just off Lhoob Doo, near Dalby Point, lies the wreck of the *Mayfield*. She had a gross weight of 4000 tons and was laden with 1800 tons of coal. She hit the rocks head-on, ripped a great seam in her hull between the main hold and the boilers and quickly settled. All the crew of 24 managed to get off in the ship's boats. After three days only her funnel was still visible. The bow of the *Mayfield* is still embedded in the rocks and, considering that she has been there since 26 September, 1909, is remarkably intact. The wreck is quite extensive and reaches way out onto the sand sea bed. The two boilers look huge under water, standing up out of the tangled girders. Some of her cargo of coal still lies scattered around and a number of us can vouch for the fact that it still burns well!

WHAT TO LOOK FOR: Although most of the cargo was salvaged, some coal remains. Edible crabs, ling and conger eels are all quite common.

OTHER INFORMATION: Negligible current. Of the two boilers, one stands upright, about 4m high, whilst the other lies horizontally. *Site map:* page 36.

Opposite: View from the footpath above the Heifers

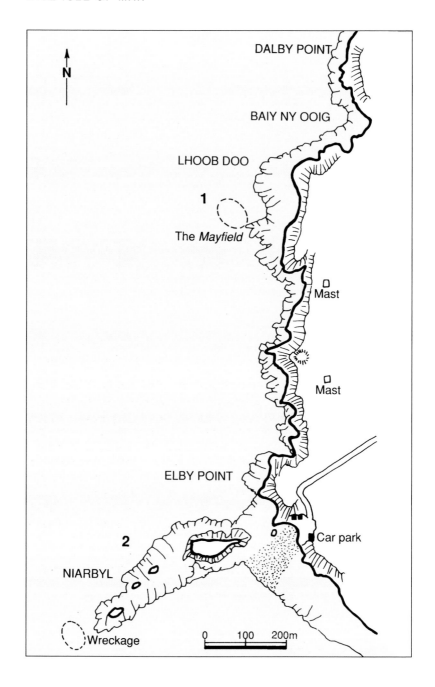

N

DALBY POINT

BAIY NY OOIG

LHOOB DOO

1

The *Mayfield*

Mast

Mast

ELBY POINT

2

Car park

NIARBYL

Wreckage

0   100   200m

2 Niarbyl

Position – SC 210 775. *Type of Dive* – Scenic. *Level of Dive* – Novice Diver. *Access* – Shore Dive or Boat Dive (launch Peel or Port Erin). *Max Depth* – 15m.

DESCRIPTION: Niarbyl means "tails of rocks" and this tail runs seawards for some 300m. The rocks meet the sand at about 10m with many small gullies. Another pleasant shore dive from Niarbyl beach is along the north side, Elby Point (SC 210 777). Best dived around the top half of the tide.

WHAT TO LOOK FOR: Crabs and many varieties of small marine life in the gullies. There is wreckage from two boats at the tip of Niarbyl, although very little remains. Interesting brittlestar beds to the SW.

OTHER INFORMATION: The rocks are cut off at HW from the beach with a strong current between, so care is needed. Very limited parking by the shore although there is ample parking above the beach, and a café.

3 Thracian

Position – 54 07 73N; 004 47 05W. *Type of Dive* – Wreck. *Level of Dive* – Dive Leader. *Access* – Boat Dive (launch Port Erin). *Max Depth* – 38m.

DESCRIPTION: 2000-ton four-mast barque built 1892 and launched on the Clyde. On 14 October, 1892, while under tow by the *Sarah Joliffe* to Liverpool to be fitted out, she started to heel over during a gale, the tow was cut and she sank. All on board were lost: the captain, his wife and the crew of Liverpool "riggers". The *Thracian* now lies upside-down on her port side, bow SW and stern NE. The masts and most of the wreckage can be found on the east side of the wreck. Much of the hull is now very thin and there are many gaps between the ribs. In 1992, to mark the centenary of the sinking, the authors, assisted by Mike Bates, Tom Dickie and Peter Astell-Burt, photographed and filmed the wreck for the descendants of Captain and Mrs Brown.

WHAT TO LOOK FOR: Stern and rudder very pretty, with framework covered in plumose anemones. Huge anchor and numerous chains and ropes. Many enormous conger eels are to be found (if you're feeling brave) in all the broken masts and spars.

Opposite: Niarbyl and the *Mayfield*

The SS *Mayfield*, 1909 (site **1**)

OTHER INFORMATION: Slack water is around HW and LW, being approximately 1hr either side on neaps. Strong surface currents are not present on the bottom. Occasionally buoyed. No brass as she sank before fitting – so leave your hammer behind!

East transit good. Place third telegraph pole in bottom of "V" between hills. Line this transit up and head in or out. Wreck 6 to 7m proud, distinctive hull shape, surrounding sea bed flat.

4 Don Bosco and Our Lassie

Position – 54 07 47N; 004 46 98W and 54 07 46N; 004 47 09W. *Type of Dive* – Wreck. *Level of Dive* – Dive Leader. *Access* – Boat Dive (launch Port Erin). *Max Depth* – 38m.

DESCRIPTION: Two trawlers collided November 1990 and sank within 300m of each other. The *Don Bosco* – a 15m steel trawler – is sitting upright on sandy sea bed. It is quite intact although some salvage has been carried out. *Our Lassie* – a 12m wooden trawler – is quite broken up, having been dredged over soon after sinking! Propellers from both boats have been raised.

WHAT TO LOOK FOR: Quite a lot of silt can easily be kicked up although it is soon removed by the current. Several nets and ropes present on the *Don Bosco*.

38

OTHER INFORMATION: A group of students at the Port Erin Marine Laboratory own the *Our Lassie* and regulate diving on the *Don Bosco*. Anyone wishing to dive either of these wrecks should contact the Diving Officer of the Port Erin Marine Biologists' Sub-Aqua Club (tel. 01624 832027).

Slack water is around HW and LW, being about 1hr either side on neaps. Strong surface currents, but weaker on the bottom. Occasionally buoyed.

5 Fleshwick Bay

Position – SC 202 716. *Type of Dive* – Scenic. *Level of Dive* – Novice Diver. *Access* – Shore dive or boat (launch Port Erin). *Max Depth* – 12m.

DESCRIPTION: Fleshwick Bay faces north and is therefore a good place to dive when the winds are strong and southerly. Best dived around HW to save the hike over slippery cobbles. The west side of the bay, towards the headland, is the better dive – snorkel the first section over the shallow wrack-covered bottom. The right hand side below the steep cliff is excellent for snorkelling with a spectacular archway in the rocks some 200m out.

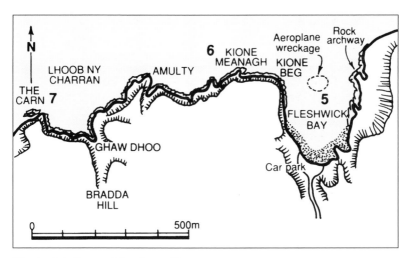

Fleshwick Bay to Lhoob ny Charran

WHAT TO LOOK FOR: Good site for all types of fish, around the rocks and on the sand in the middle of the bay and around the headland. Lots of hermit crabs. Aeroplane wreckage has been seen in the middle of the bay.

OTHER INFORMATION: There are no currents within the bay and only a slight current around the headland. If shore diving, take the road from Port Erin that loops around Rowany Golf Course and follow the road signposted for Fleshwick. There is limited parking at Fleshwick and access is over a cobbled beach (hence best dived around HW).

6 Kione Meanagh

Position – SC 199 717. *Type of Dive* – Scenic. *Level of Dive* – Sports Diver. *Access* – Boat Dive (launch Port Erin). *Max Depth* – 18m.

DESCRIPTION: Around the corner from Fleshwick the underwater cliffs are steep and make an excellent dive. Facing due north they tend to be dark – so take a torch to investigate the many crevices.

WHAT TO LOOK FOR: Numerous conger eels between here and Amulty.

OTHER INFORMATION: Apart from Kione Meanagh Point, the current flow in either direction is only 1kn maximum – good for a gentle drift. *Site map:* page 39.

7 Lhoob ny Charran

Position – SC 194 716. *Type of Dive* – Scenic. *Level of Dive* – Sports Diver. *Access* – Boat Dive (launch Port Erin). *Max Depth* – 19m.

DESCRIPTION: This small bay between the headlands of Amulty and the Carn is easily identified by Ghaw Dhoo – a large ravine on the steep hillside. Under water, the north-facing cliffs are very sheer, with overhangs. The vertical cliff wall descends to a flat sand and gravel sea bed.

WHAT TO LOOK FOR: Below the narrow kelp zone the walls are covered with masses of dead man's fingers; below these, Devonshire cup corals "stud" the cliffs and rocks in large numbers. Many fish: conger, ling, several kinds of wrasse and pollack. Take a good torch in order to explore the many ravines.

OTHER INFORMATION: On the flood tide, a current of up to 2kn may be encountered around the headlands; the current is negligible within the bay. *Site map:* page 39.

8 The Carn

Position – SC 193 716. *Type of Dive* – Scenic. *Level of Dive* – Sports Diver. *Access* – Boat Dive (launch Port Erin). *Max Depth* – 19m.

DESCRIPTION: Situated below the towering slopes of Bradda Hill there are small underwater cliffs with many small crevices and ledges. A large boulder slope leads down to a sandy sea bed with gravel and cobble patches.

WHAT TO LOOK FOR: Rich kelp community higher up and large numbers of wrasse, pollack and other fish among the boulders.

OTHER INFORMATION: Drift towards the *Citrine* (site **9**) on the flood or from the *Citrine* to the Carn on the ebb. *Site map:* page 42.

9 Citrine

Position – SC 190 712. *Type of Dive* – Wreck. *Level of Dive* – Novice Diver. *Access* – Boat Dive (launch Port Erin). *Max Depth* – 16m.

DESCRIPTION: Built in 1921 at Aberdeen, the SS *Citrine*, a 165-foot coaster weighing 650 tons, ran aground in thick fog on the evening of 17 March, 1931. It was quite a disaster, with ten men drowned. Only two managed to swim to the safety of the rocks in the dark. Not knowing where they were,

The wreckage of the SS *Citrine*, north of Port Erin

41

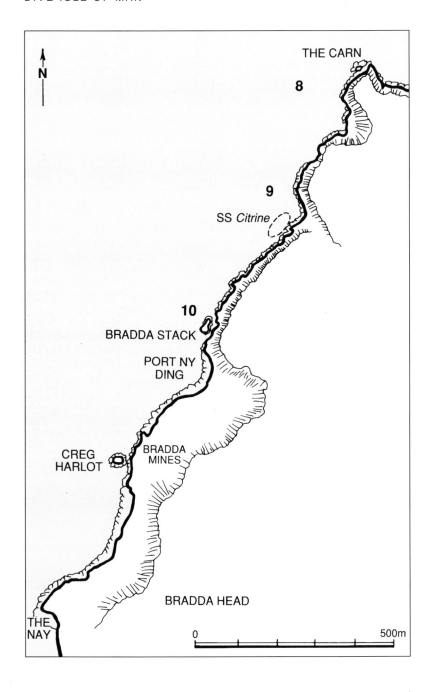

N

THE CARN

8

9

SS *Citrine*

10

BRADDA STACK

PORT NY
DING

CREG
HARLOT

BRADDA
MINES

BRADDA HEAD

THE
NAY

0   500m

they had to wait until first light and then climb the very steep cliffs of Bradda Head and find a cottage to raise the alarm. The *Citrine* now lies just a mile north of Port Erin, close to the cliffs and along the bottom of the rock line. The boiler and engine stand clear of the wreckage, which includes propeller, winches and a fairly intact bow section with anchor, chains and the spare propeller. The *Citrine* lies with her bow south and stern north.

WHAT TO LOOK FOR: Very pleasant novice dive – usually good visibility. Dense patches of plumose anemones and dead man's fingers. Friendly wrasse wait to greet divers, hoping that they will stir up some food.

OTHER INFORMATION: May be dived at most states of tide – slight current for 2hrs after HW but less than 1kn.

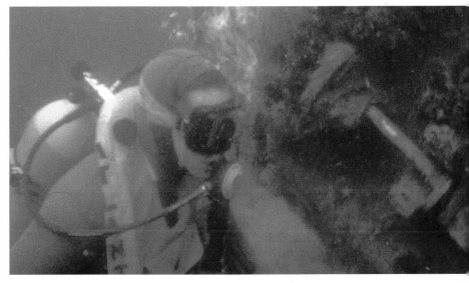

Part of the engine of the popular *Citrine* wreck (site **9**)

Opposite: The Carn to Bradda Head

43

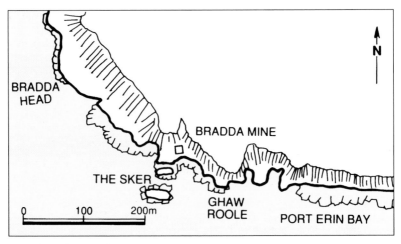

The Sker (site **11**)

10 Bradda Stack

Position – SC 188 709. *Type of Dive* – Scenic/Drift. *Level of Dive* – Novice Diver/Sports Diver. *Access* – Boat Dive (launch Port Erin). *Max Depth* – 15m.

DESCRIPTION: A safe site for novice diving – shallow and gentle currents. Kelp covered boulder slope descends to the gravel and rocky bottom. Diving around the stack reveals several superb caves; for example a tunnel behind the stack, about 8m long, 3m wide and in 6m (at LW). Alternatively drift along the base of the cliff, south towards Port Erin or north onto the wreck of the *Citrine* (site **9**).

WHAT TO LOOK FOR: Numerous anemones may be found within the gullies and caves, and a rich kelp community.

OTHER INFORMATION: Very little current – less than 2kn on spring tides. *Site map:* page 42.

11 The Sker

Position – SC 184 697. *Type of Dive* – Scenic. *Level of Dive* – Novice Diver. *Access* – Boat Dive (launch Port Erin). *Max Depth* – 18m.

DESCRIPTION: Two different dives, depending on whether you turn into or out of the bay. Both dives start at the point of the Sker. Enter the water as close to the rock as conditions will allow, just inside the outer point. The rock face terminates in about 6m. Heading west, out of the bay, will bring you to a gully lined with plumose anemones. From here turn south and follow the boulder slope down to the sand/gravel at 16 to 18m. Follow this margin of large boulders on sand/gravel. Another dive may be had by turning east into the bay at the bottom of the rock face and following it around towards the mine chimney. Again, head south into deeper water and then follow the sand/boulder margin into the bay.

WHAT TO LOOK FOR: Plumose anemones, dead man's fingers, octopus, dogfish, wrasse, plaice, spiny starfish, sponges and nudibranchs.

OTHER INFORMATION: The area from the point of the Sker is exposed to current that can run at two knots on spring tides. Slack is centred around half tide and can be up to two hours at neaps. There is no significant current inside the bay.

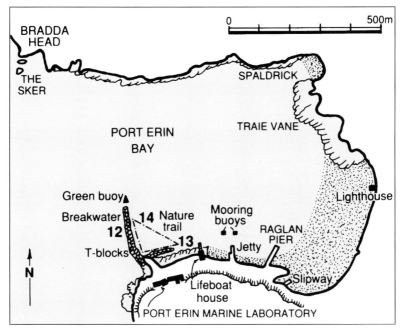

Port Erin Bay

12 The Breakwater

Position – SC 188 690. *Type of Dive* – Scenic. *Level of Dive* – Novice Diver. *Access* – Shore dive (breakwater steps). *Max Depth* – 15m.

DESCRIPTION: This must be the best known and most popular dive on the Isle of Man. It is the ruins of a large breakwater built in 1876 and subsequently destroyed by the winter storms of 1879 and 1882. The huge scattered blocks now create a superb site that has attracted a multitude of marine organisms. To complete a trip right around takes approximately 45 minutes – dive or snorkel over the top of the breakwater to the outside and then follow the blocks. It is slightly deeper on the outside of the breakwater and a current flowing in and out of the bay is noticeable at the north (far) end of the breakwater, near the green buoy. Also, the nature trail runs along the inside of the breakwater.

WHAT TO LOOK FOR: Thousands of sea-urchins graze on the kelp growing on the blocks. Wrasse of all kinds, conger eels, pollack, topknot and bib are abundant. The wrasse are particularly tame. Also numerous plumose anemones and dead man's fingers.

Port Erin breakwater at low water, with the blocks showing; Bradda Head and the Sker Rocks in the distance

OTHER INFORMATION: Port Erin Marine Laboratory has several experiments under progress within the bay. By all means look, but please do not touch or interfere with them. Take care entering from the breakwater steps at LW as the bottom steps are broken and unsafe. Care must also be taken on exiting when there is a surge around the steps. *Site map:* page 45.

13 The T-blocks – "Crab Row" to Port Erin Jetty

Position – SC 188 690 to 192 690. *Type of Dive* – Scenic. *Level of Dive* – Novice Diver. *Access* – Shore dive (via jetty or breakwater steps). *Max Depth* – 12m.

DESCRIPTION: The T-blocks were once the inner arm of the breakwater, so named because of their shape. Very sheltered from all but W to SW winds – dive at low water as the breakwater provides considerable shelter. On entering by the breakwater steps, descend the steep boulder slope to the bottom of the bay and head east, towards the jetty. The inner leg of the nature trail also runs along these blocks. At the end, carry on parallel to the large boulders, past the lifeboat slip to the jetty.

WHAT TO LOOK FOR: Many fish, including ballan, cuckoo and corkwing wrasse, topknot, conger eel, bib and pipefish. Numerous crabs, and at night hundreds of spiny squat lobsters. Superb for night dives.

OTHER INFORMATION: Port Erin Marine Laboratory has several experiments under progress within the bay. By all means look, but please do not touch or interfere with these experiments. Take care entering from the breakwater steps at LW as the bottom steps are broken and unsafe. *Site map:* page 45.

14 Nature Trail

Position – SC 188 690. *Type of Dive* – Scenic. *Level of Dive* – Novice Diver. *Access* – Shore dive (from jetty or breakwater). *Max Depth* – 14m.

DESCRIPTION: The nature trail follows an angular course starting opposite the steps at the base of the ruined breakwater. The guide rope follows these remains, on the shore side heading north for about 200m before turning into the bay and crossing the sand to join the remains of the old jetty known as the T-blocks. It follows the blocks back to the start point. The total distance is about 600m and a complete circuit, allowing time for observation, takes nearly an hour. There is a visitors' book about a third of the way across the sand from the breakwater. A shorter version of the nature trail may be undertaken by turning southward about 20m after the visitors' book at a work site set up by the Port Erin Marine Laboratory (please do not touch), following the guide rope back to the T-blocks.

WHAT TO LOOK FOR: Forest kelp, sugar kelp, oarweed, furbelows and dabberlocks. Wrasse, plaice, topknot, bib, pouting, pipefish, dogfish and conger eels. Dead man's fingers, Devonshire cup corals, snakelocks, dahlia and plumose anemones. Sea-urchin, spiny starfish, bloody henry, featherstars, common starfish and sunstar. Peacock worms, velvet crabs, edible crabs, squat lobsters and octopus.

OTHER INFORMATION: Further details from Port Erin Commissioners or from Mike Bates at the Marine Laboratory. Tel: 01624 832027. *Site map: page 45.*

15 Ringwall

Position – 54 07 06N; 004 53 39W. *Type of Dive* – Wreck. *Level of Dive* – Dive Leader/Advanced Diver. *Access* – Boat Dive (launch Port Erin). *Max Depth* – 46m.

DESCRIPTION: This steel steamship of 407 tons (formerly the *Mary Summerville*, 143ft long with a beam of 25ft, left Dublin in ballast on 27 January, 1941, bound for Silloth. It hit a mine and was lost with its eight crew. It sits upright on the sandy sea bed, and is quite intact apart from the wooden wheelhouse that soon broke up and a hole presumably caused by the mine.

WHAT TO LOOK FOR: Site is 4.8nm west of Port Erin (on a bearing of about 290°) and should be undertaken only in a reliable boat and with a good weather forecast. Small amount of net present mid-ship. Very large conger eels and ling. Occasionally buoyed by the Port Erin Marine Biologists' Sub-Aqua Club.

OTHER INFORMATION: Strong current on spring tides – often pulls the marking buoy under. Surface and bottom current up to 2kn but good slack for 2½ to 1½hrs before HW and 3 to 4hrs after HW (similar to the Calf Sound). Quite a lot of silt in the stern section easily stirred up. The orientation of the wreck is NW/SE.

16 Creg Liauyr
Position – SC 186 686. *Type of Dive* – Scenic. *Level of Dive* – Novice Diver. *Access* – Boat Dive (launch Port Erin). *Max Depth* – 18m.

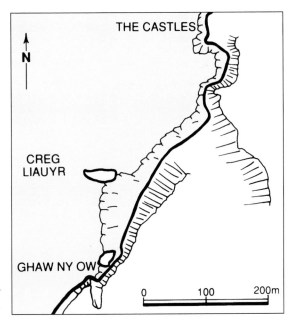

THE CASTLES

N

CREG
LIAUYR

GHAW NY OW

0   100   200m

Creg Liauyr
(site **16**)

DESCRIPTION: A shallow bay with its limits marked by large rock formations; exposed at the NE end and submerged at the SW end. Between these points is a mass of large and small boulders on bedrock and covered in kelp, which form a wide shelf about 8m deep, before dropping in a jumble of large boulders to about 16m. Here the boulders end at a gently sloping sand/gravel sea bed with small stones and boulders. Vertical faces, deep and shallow, occur on the rocks at both ends of the bay, but the face at the SW end is larger and bears a greater variety of life.

WHAT TO LOOK FOR: Kelp forest and associated fauna in the shallow areas. Large sea-urchin population deeper; greatest at NE end where the highest population in the Isle of Man has been recorded. Dead man's fingers and plumose anemones, the latter more common at the SW end where it extends onto the stones in deeper water. Sponges, nudibranchs, wrasse, octopus and crabs.

OTHER INFORMATION: The inshore side of the bay is sheltered from the main tides and consequently current is not a problem. Further offshore, the current can run at about 1kn (2kn on spring tides). Slack is at half tide and can vary from 2hrs (neap tides) to half an hour (spring tides).

17 Bay Fine

Position – SC 182 680. *Type of Dive* – Scenic. *Level of Dive* – Sports Diver. *Access* – Boat Dive (launch Port Erin). *Max Depth* – 22m.

DESCRIPTION: A relatively sheltered and shallow NW-facing bay bounded by steep cliffs. Boulder slopes and rocky gullies descend to a coarse sand and pebble bottom in 15 to 20m.

WHAT TO LOOK FOR: The marine life is diverse and plentiful, due to the absence of dredging within the bay. Large numbers of featherstars, brittlestars, burrowing anemones, crabs, prawns, shrimp and fish. The prolific fauna within this undredged bay provokes a sobering thought as to the damage inflicted to regular fishing areas. Some 15m off the SW corner of Bay Fine is a large underwater outcrop, Stack Fine, standing 15m proud of the sea bed at 18m HW. It has sheer sides and is covered with life: the N face is a mass of white plumose anemones.

OTHER INFORMATION: Bay Fine is extensively used by Port Erin Marine Laboratory for scallop aquaculture. A large buoyed rope system exists at the south end of the bay and should be avoided. Tides are very localised and not at all predictable, but run at no more than 2kn.

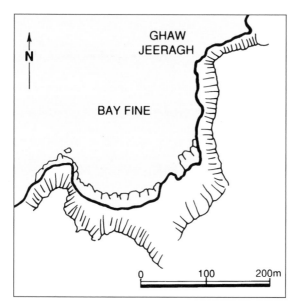

Bay Fine (site **17**)

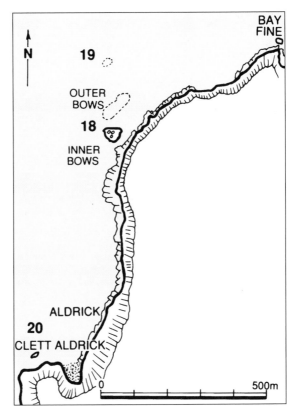

The Outer Bows to Clett Aldrick

18 Inner Bows or Halfway Rocks

Position – SC 177 678. *Type of Dive* – Scenic/Drift. *Level of Dive* – Sports Diver. *Access* – Boat Dive (launch Port Erin). *Max Depth* – 25m.

DESCRIPTION: Rock outcrop 1 mile SW of Port Erin. Very pleasant dive with a vertical wall on the Calf side of the large exposed rock. Both sides are very interesting with large slate slabs and other outcrops. Running west is a low formation of boulders at approximately 25m.

WHAT TO LOOK FOR: Diverse marine life on the rock walls. Devonshire cup corals and hydroids are common. Fish life is particularly prolific with many conger eels on the south side.

OTHER INFORMATION: Fairly strong tide on the flood so it is best dived on an ebb or slack tide. Slack 2¹/₂ to 1¹/₂hrs before HW and 3 to 4hrs after HW. Slack tide times are the same as in the Calf Sound.

19 Outer Bows

Position – SC 177 679. *Type of Dive* – Scenic/Drift. *Level of Dive* – Sports Diver/Dive Leader. *Access* – Boat Dive (launch Port Erin). *Max Depth* – 25m.

DESCRIPTION: Large outcrop of rocks approximately 75m west of the Inner Bows (site **18**). They rise from the sandy sea bed at 22m to within 7 to 8m (LW) of the surface at the SW end. The rocks that make up the Outer Bows can be circumnavigated in 35 to 40 minutes.

WHAT TO LOOK FOR: The vertical cliffs support dense colonies of white plumose anemones on the SW end. It is a high-energy site with a good variety of hydroids.

OTHER INFORMATION: Dive at slack water (slack is 2¹/₂ to 1¹/₂hrs before HW and 3 to 4hrs after HW) as the current is too strong for divers to stay on the rocky outcrop during the flood tide. *Site map:* page 51.

20 Aldrick

Position – SC 674 175. *Type of Dive* – Scenic. *Level of Dive* – Sports Diver. *Access* – Boat Dive (launch Port Erin). *Max Depth* – 20m.

DESCRIPTION: Sheer cliffs protect this dive site from the wind and the bay is free of strong currents. Massive slabs and lintels are a main feature of the steep rock walls, very similar to the area between Spanish Head and Black Head. The sea bed is flat sand.

WHAT TO LOOK FOR: Lots of life lurking under the huge rocks – take a torch.

OTHER INFORMATION: Strong currents outside the bay, particularly on the flood tide. *Site map:* page 51.

21 The Heifers (Im Laud) and Clett Aldrick

Position – SC 173 670 and 174 672. *Type of Dive* – Scenic/Drift. *Level of Dive* – Sports Diver/Dive Leader. *Access* – Boat Dive (launch Port Erin). *Max Depth* – 25m.

DESCRIPTION: Clett Aldrick is an exposed rock lying at the base of a small headland below the steep cliffs. The Heifers are a small outcrop of rocks showing at most states of the tide, some 200m SW of Clett Aldrick. Drift dive from one site to another or make separate dives at slack tide – take time to explore the many gullies.

WHAT TO LOOK FOR: A high energy site with plenty of life. Many fish with conger eels in crevices. Many encrusting creatures on the rocks, anemones such as *Actinothoë*, and hydroids.

OTHER INFORMATION: Strong tides present, particularly on the flood. Pick slack – times as per Calf Sound (slack $2^{1}/_{2}$ to $1^{1}/_{2}$hrs before HW and 3 to 4hrs after HW) or ebb when the run is less. *Site map:* page 51.

THE CALF OF MAN

Off the south-west tip of the Isle of Man lies the Calf of Man. It is separated by the fast-flowing Calf Sound, which has other navigational hazards: the islet Kitterland and Thousla Rock. The Calf of Man is about a mile across and is the property of the Manx National Trust. The residents are the lighthouse keepers who live in the most modern of the three lighthouses and, in the summer, a warden who observes and documents the thousands of nesting and visiting birds. There is also a flock of the Manx native breed of sheep, the four-horned Loghtan. There are two main harbours, Cow Harbour and South Harbour. The rest of the Calf consists of steep cliffs.

This area covers dive sites around the Calf of Man and includes the Calf Sound and Chicken Rock.

22 Calf Sound

Position – SC 168 665. *Type of Dive* – Scenic/Drift. *Level of Dive* – Sports Diver/Dive Leader. *Access* – Boat Dive (launch Port Erin or Port St Mary). *Max Depth* – 30m.

DESCRIPTION: Wickedly fast drift dive. Best dived NW to SE. Drop in approximately 50m NE of Thousla Rock and descend rapidly. Calf Sound bottom covered in dead man's fingers and plumose anemones – like a garden! Depth range 18 to 26m. Boulders mostly smaller than 1m and provide shelter for fish. Current determines distance covered. Once through the Sound, the current drops. Gravel/sand further offshore. An alternative dive is to drop onto the *Clan MacMaster* (site **23**) if the current is not too strong and then enter the Sound.

WHAT TO LOOK FOR: The bottom of the Sound is densely covered with dead man's fingers and plumose anemones, which are very pretty – well worth taking a camera along. Ross coral at the base of Thousla rock. Lots of wreckage is strewn along the bottom; this and the boulders provide numerous habitats for crabs, lobsters and wrasse.

OTHER INFORMATION: Slack water is $2^1/_2$ to $1^1/_2$hrs before HW and 3 to 4hrs after HW. Maximum current for drifting is from 1 to 2hrs after HW and 4 to 5hrs before HW and up to 4 to 6 knots on spring tides. Great care must be taken in order not to drift between Thousla Rock and the Calf of Man as this channel is shallow (less than 5m) and fast flowing. Also do not go too far east of Thousla Rock as the currents tend to travel around the southern edge of Kitterland – again, fast and shallow.

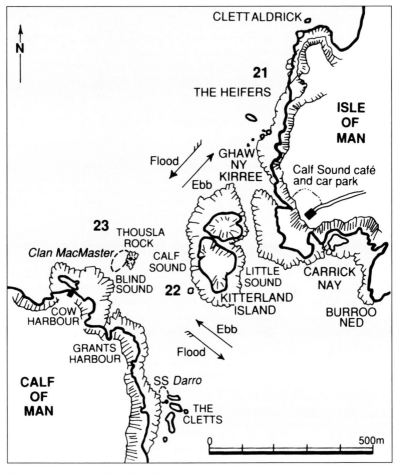

The area around the Calf Sound

The Calf Sound. Only small, shallow-draught craft can go through the Little Sound at high water. The main channel is on the far side of Kitterland

23 Clan MacMaster

Position – SC 168 665. *Type of Dive* – Wreck. *Level of Dive* – Sports Diver. *Access* – Boat Dive (launch Port Erin or Port St Mary). *Max Depth* – 25m.

DESCRIPTION: On 30 September, 1923, the *Clan MacMaster* grounded in the Calf Sound during thick fog that caused 17 vessels to be wrecked in British waters. Launched in Sunderland on 24 February, 1917, the 6563-ton, 420-ft Clan Line steamer was the largest vessel to be wrecked on the Isle of Man. She was carrying a cargo of over 3000 tons: cars, sewing machines, other machinery, cotton and coal. Even so, she was only partially laden, on her way to Liverpool for more cargo before sailing for the East.

The crew of 80 men all managed to get off the ship alive and without injury. Much of the cargo was salvaged before the winter storms and many a household in the south of the island had – and still has – a sewing machine from this wreck. The *Clan MacMaster* ran onto a reef of rocks known locally as the Blind Sound (being not the part of the Sound used for navigation). She now lies right across the west side of Thousla Rock, which has a navigation mark (white tower) on top, in the middle of the Calf Sound. Some sections are in deeper water in the main channel of the

Sound. Although well broken up, the wreckage is extensive. Large numbers of fish hang around the tall wreckage in the Blind Sound, darting for cover when a seal is on the hunt.

WHAT TO LOOK FOR: Best to dive her by dropping in 10 to 20m west off Thousla Rock and descending rapidly. Prop shaft is at the bottom of Thousla Rock and can be followed South to the engines and huge boilers. Large shoals of fish and many seals. White plumose anemones and Devonshire cup corals on Thousla Rock.

OTHER INFORMATION: Care must be taken when diving this wreck. Select neap tides and arrive in good time for slack water, which is $2^1/_2$ to $1^1/_2$hrs before HW and 3 to 4hrs after HW. An alternative is to initially dive the wreck but then enter the Sound (site **22**). Take care not to be washed through the Blind Sound as it is very shallow (less than 5m in places) and the current very strong.

24 Gibdale Bay and the Incentive

Position – SC 160 663. *Type of Dive* – Scenic/Drift/Wreck. *Level of Dive* – Novice Diver/Sports Diver. *Access* – Boat Dive (launch Port Erin or Port St Mary). *Max Depth* – 20m.

One of the many friendly seals

The *Clan MacMaster* grounded in Calf Sound, 1923 (site **23**)

DESCRIPTION: North-facing bay on the Calf of Man. High cliffs provide quite a lot of shelter from S, SW and W winds although Gibdale Point may be rough. Gibdale Bay is easily located as there is a small birdwatching hut halfway up the cliff. The actual bay is shallow (6 to 8m) and consists of large boulders and rocks on bedrock. Dense kelp forest. Pretty and safe for novice diving.

There is a steep slope of very large boulders some 100m offshore that descends from 8m to 16m. The slope runs onto sand and gravel, and here are the remains of the *Mary Barrow*, a three-masted schooner with cargo of coal and wrecked in 1938 – but very broken. The *Incentive* was an 25m Irish trawler that went aground in 1978. Engine and some spars visible at LW. Many plates, bits of trawling gear, winches and other items may be found in shallow water close inshore.

WHAT TO LOOK FOR: Prolific marine life. Brittlestar beds offshore on the sand, kelp forests within the bay and lots of dead man's fingers, plumose anemones and sponges towards the point. Keep a look out for seals.

OTHER INFORMATION: Well sheltered, with negligible current inside the bay. Stronger currents can occur around the point. *Site map:* page 62.

Opposite: Tide times for the Calf of Man (spring tides) – the key to the numbers on the map is as follows:

1. Slack water in Calf Sound – 2½ to 1½hrs before HW and 3 to 4hrs after HW. The flood runs easterly; the ebb runs westerly.

2. Drift diving in Calf Sound – 1 to 2hrs after HW (south to north) and 4 to 5hrs before HW (north to south).

3. From Kione Beg the tide runs towards The Stack continuously, except from 1½hrs before HW to HW, when the tide runs from The Stack to Kione Beg.

4. Slack on The Stack – 1½hrs before HW to HW.

5. Tides between Chicken Rock lighthouse and the Calf run full range as per Liverpool (see above). Tides are strong, especially on Chicken Rock, The Stack, Caigher Point and The Burroo. Tides are not predictable close inshore between The Stack and Caigher Point, with eddies and frequent tidal changes. This also occurs in The Puddle, where the tide is not as strong inshore.

6. Slack on Chicken Rock – 1¼hrs before HW to HW and 4 to 5hrs after HW. The LW slack is preferable.

7. Slack on The Burroo – 1½hrs before LW to LW.

8. Tide runs from The Burroo towards Ghaw Yiarn for 1hr before LW to 1 hr after LW; then from Ghaw Yiarn to The Burroo until the next LW.

9. From Spanish Head close inshore to Kallow Point, slack water is 2½ to 1½hrs before HW and 3 to 4hrs after HW. The flood runs easterly; the ebb runs westerly. Tides can be strong, especially at Spanish Head, Black Head, Sugarloaf, Kione y Ghoggan and Kallow Point. Slack water is very brief during spring tides.

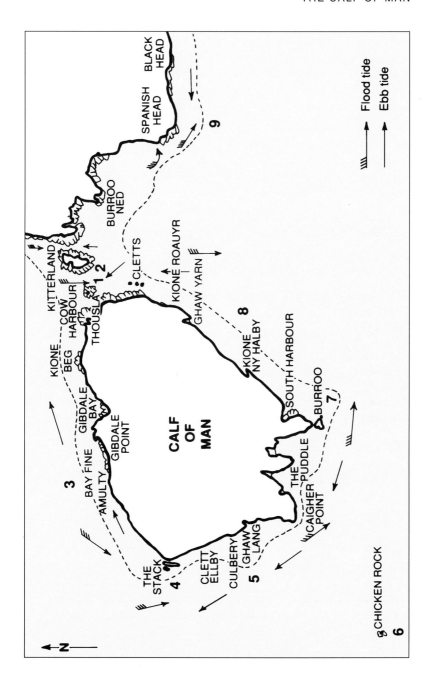

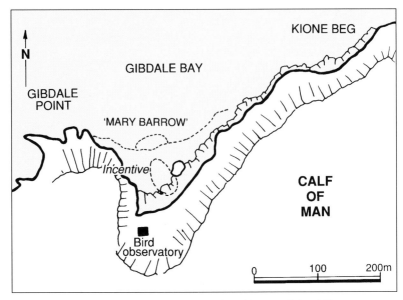

Gibdale Bay, the *Incentive* and the *Mary Barrow* (site **24**)

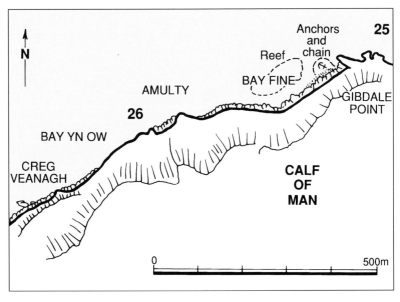

Gibdale Point and Amulty

25 Gibdale Point

Position – SC 158 663. *Type of Dive* – Scenic/Drift/Wreck. *Level of Dive* – Novice Diver/Sports Diver. *Access* – Boat Dive (launch Port Erin or Port St Mary). *Max Depth* – 25m. *Site map:* page 62.

DESCRIPTION: Gibdale Point is a very scenic dive with many vertical faces, gullies and several caves. In addition, there is a large amount of chain and huge anchors from a "semi-wreck". On the morning of 14 May, 1911, the SS *Greatham* ran aground just south of Gibdale Point in thick fog. The rock on which she was stranded was blown away and her anchors and chain dumped overboard to lighten the bow. With the assistance of the SS *Ranger* the *Greatham* was finally re-floated on 22 May, 1914. The anchors are huge (2m high and over 3m long) and enormous piles of chain lie nearby, close inshore in 6 to 8m. A steep boulder slope leads down from the anchor site to a reef situated towards the NW end of Bay Fine.

WHAT TO LOOK FOR: Seals are very common. Prolific marine life with numerous dead man's fingers, plumose anemones, sea lemons, sea hares and sponges around the point and on the reef. Many wrasse on the reef.

OTHER INFORMATION: Strong currents can occur around the point and offshore on the reef, however it is quite sheltered close inshore.

26 Amulty

Position – SC 154 662. *Type of Dive* – Scenic/Drift. *Level of Dive* – Sports Diver. *Access* – Boat Dive (launch Port Erin or Port St Mary). *Max Depth* – 25m.

DESCRIPTION: Very scenic dive. Large rocky outcrops, small cliffs and gullies down to sand/gravel in about 20m. Many huge boulders covered with marine organisms. Very pretty drift dive over the small reefs scattered amongst the sand.

WHAT TO LOOK FOR: Anemones, crabs and lobsters are common as are seals. The reefs are covered with white plumose anemones in dense beds.

OTHER INFORMATION: The tide runs SW towards the Stack for about 4½hrs in each 6hr cycle. Negligible effect close in but 1 to 2kn over the sand/gravel. Avoid drifting too close to the Stack otherwise you will be sucked through! Not advisable unless planned – a good time to use an SMB – but take care not to get caught up in the numerous pot lines.

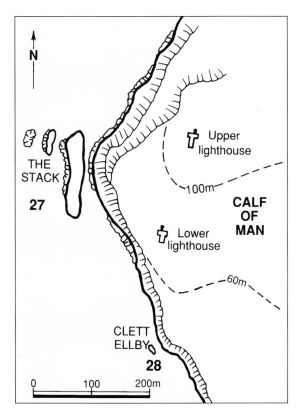

The Stack and Clett Ellby – dotted lines indicate contours

27 The Stack

Position – SC 148 656. *Type of Dive* – Drift/Scenic. *Level of Dive* – Dive Leader. *Access* – Boat Dive (launch Port Erin or Port St Mary). *Max Depth* – 30m.

DESCRIPTION: Large rock outcrop on the west side of the Calf. Several other pinnacles are present running parallel to the main outcrop. Best to drop in 20 to 30m north off the Stack rock, descend rapidly and swim (or drift!) south.

WHAT TO LOOK FOR: The marine life on the Stack is similar to the other exposed sites of the Calf of Man (the Burroo and Chicken Rock, for example). All the cliff faces are covered in dense communities of encrusting organisms such as dead man's fingers, plumose anemones, jewel anemones, hydroids, hornwrack and sponges. Many fish and seals.

OTHER INFORMATION: The tide runs towards the Stack continuously except from 1¹/₂hrs before HW until HW. During this period it runs from the Stack to Gibdale Bay.

28 Clett Ellby

Position – SC 149 654. *Type of Dive* – Drift/Scenic. *Level of Dive* – Sports Diver. *Access* – Boat Dive (launch Port Erin or Port St Mary). *Max Depth* – 30m.

DESCRIPTION: From the steep cliffs, rock pinnacles and gullies extend underwater, descending down to a flat gravel bottom. There are some very interesting step-like reefs further offshore in about 28m.

WHAT TO LOOK FOR: There is quite a lot of kelp at shallower depths. Several caves to explore. Brittlestars and scallops on the gravel bed offshore.

The lighthouse on Chicken Rock, a favourite haul out for grey seals at low water (site **30**)

OTHER INFORMATION: Currents and slack times are similar to the those of the Stack. Possible to find sheltered conditions close inshore, but Clett Ellby is quite exposed further offshore. Eddies and backcurrents occur on spring tides.

29 Chicken Rock

Position – SC 143 639. *Type of Dive* – Scenic/Drift. *Level of Dive* – Dive Leader/Advanced Diver. *Access* – Boat Dive (launch Port Erin or Port St Mary). *Max Depth* – 50m.

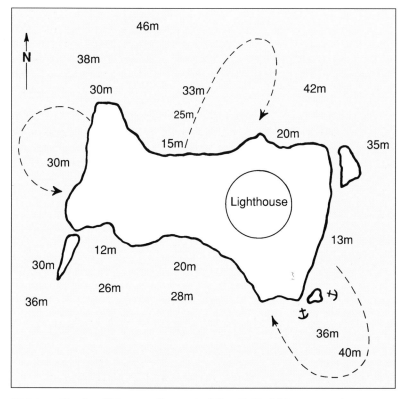

Chicken Rock, off the south-west of the Calf of Man – numbers indicate approximate depths at low water (site **29**)

DESCRIPTION: Chicken Rock lies three-quarters of a mile SW of the Calf. The lighthouse was built in 1875. An exposed site with very strong and sometimes unpredictable currents.

Drop in within the small bay N or NE of the lighthouse. Descend on a bearing of 30° down the kelp-covered cliffs until the boulder slope is reached. The large rocks and overhanging boulders may be followed down to 35 to 40m where the sea bed flattens off and consists of small boulders and bedrock covered with dead man's fingers. Return to Chicken Rock on a bearing of 210°. Another dive can be undertaken by heading south around the rock and then offshore – 25m vertical drop-offs are present on the southern tip.

WHAT TO LOOK FOR: The marine life is abundant and, as fishermen rarely place pots around the rock, there are many crabs. Please leave. The seals on the rock are very tame and often play with divers, including biting fins. Plumose anemones and dead man's fingers are large and very common, as are "sheets" of the jewel anemone and large mats of hydroids. An extensive amount of wreckage has been found on Chicken Rock: lead ingots, brass buckles, square copper nails, one very large and several smaller anchors.

OTHER INFORMATION: This site should only be attempted at slack water. On neap tides slack water is from 2hrs to 1hr before LW. Arrive at the site well before slack and get kitted-up as slack occurs very rapidly.

30 Caigher Point

Position – SC 148 656. *Type of Dive* – Drift/Scenic. *Level of Dive* – Dive Leader/Advanced Diver. *Access* – Boat Dive (launch Port Erin or Port St Mary). *Max Depth* – 50m.

DESCRIPTION: SW tip of the Calf of Man. Steep cliffs, pinnacles and gullies drop down to a boulder slope in 15m. Heading south, the boulder slope descends at 45° and reaches 50m very quickly.

WHAT TO LOOK FOR: Sparse kelp in the shallower parts, and relatively barren cliffs. Lots of life on and around the boulders. Many wrasse.

OTHER INFORMATION: Very strong and unpredictable currents – many eddies. Slack water around 1hr before HW. *Site map:* page 69.

Close encounter with a basking shark

Basking shark feeding on plankton

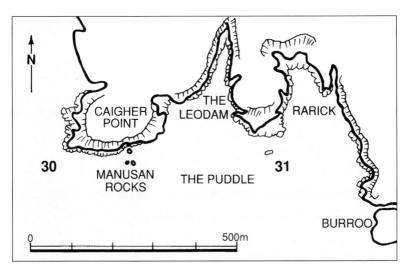

Caigher Point and The Puddle

31 The Puddle

Position – SC 156 647. *Type of Dive* – Scenic. *Level of Dive* – Novice Diver/Sports Diver. *Access* – Boat Dive (launch Port Erin or Port St Mary). *Max Depth* – 22m.

DESCRIPTION: Very sheltered bay, south-facing, that can be safely dived during most states of tide. If windy, anchor close to the cliffs. Cliffs descend to 10 to 15m; at the base is a gentle slope of very large boulders and rocks in gullies leading to a flat sand bottom.

WHAT TO LOOK FOR: Watch out for large submerged rocks off the Puddle tip – normally occupied by seals! Lots of kelp, wrasse, crabs, sponges and anemones. Keep an eye open for inquisitive seals. Some interesting wreckage has been found here over the years including a bell and cannon, but no actual wreck site located. Keep your eyes open!

OTHER INFORMATION: No noticeable current, but great care must be taken if diving south along the east wall towards the Burroo (site **32**) as very strong currents are normally present. Take an SMB!

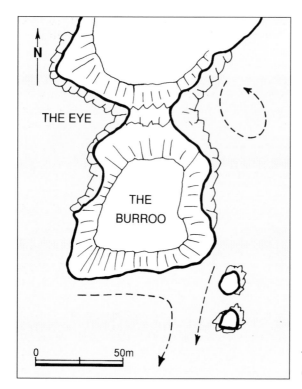

The Burroo
(site **32**)

32 The Burroo

Position – SC 159 645. *Type of Dive* – Scenic/Drift. *Level of Dive* – Sports Diver/Dive Leader. *Access* – Boat Dive (launch Port Erin or Port St Mary). *Max Depth* – 40m.

DESCRIPTION: Several spectacular dives can be made on the Burroo, an impressive rocky outcrop at the southern tip of the Calf of Man. Underwater life is prolific and it has been described as one of the best dive sites in the Irish Sea. Vertical cliffs descend to 12m, then gullies and large boulders descend gently to sand/gravel in 35m or more. There are a few large wooden beams wedged in the gullies: possibly remains of the *Young Holliday*, wrecked while travelling back from America with a cargo of cotton around 1840 – one of several boats wrecked off here.

WHAT TO LOOK FOR: The cliffs are totally covered with marine life such as jewel anemones, sponges, Devonshire cup corals and dead man's fingers. Good site for seal spotting.

OTHER INFORMATION: Best slack water is 1¹/₂hrs before LW to LW. Can be dived at slack water by sport divers or as drift for more experienced divers. An exceptionally pretty drift dive is achieved by dropping in 50 to 100m east of the outlying rocks, descending fast and then drifting SW towards Chicken Rock (2 to 3kn and up to 35m).

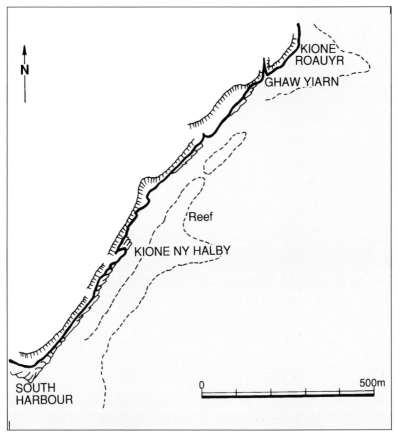

Kione ny Halby (site **33**)

33 Kione ny Halby

Position – SC 164 652. *Type of Dive* – Scenic/Drift. *Level of Dive* – Sports Diver. *Access* – Boat Dive (launch Port Erin or Port St Mary). *Max Depth* – 25m.

DESCRIPTION: A very scenic dive along a 45° slope of large rocks and boulders, some standing quite high and covered in sessile creatures. At the bottom of the slope on the sand and gravel sea bed lies a reef that runs parallel to the shore.

WHAT TO LOOK FOR: Lots of fish: pollack, conger eels, ling, saithe. The reef is covered in dead man's fingers, hydroids and various anemones.

OTHER INFORMATION: Sheltered from W and NW winds, this section of the Calf is best dived on the flood tide when the current is minimum. The ebb tide can be very strong and flows towards the Burroo, therefore drift from the Cletts to South Harbour – fast! *Site map:* page 71.

Sargartia elegans var. *rosea*

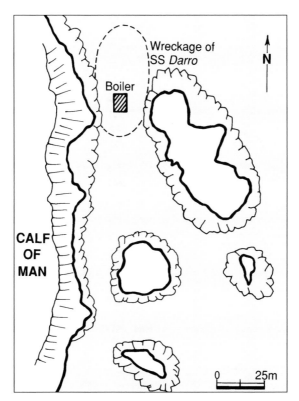

The Cletts and the wreckage of the *Darro* (site **34**)

34 The Cletts and the Darro

Position – SC 169 661. *Type of Dive* – Scenic/Wreck. *Level of Dive* – Novice Diver/Sports Diver. *Access* – Boat Dive (launch Port Erin or Port St Mary). *Max Depth* – 12m.

DESCRIPTION: A small group of rocks on the far east side of the Calf of Man, barely exposed at HW but very prominent at LW. A haul out site for seals – care must be taken as they are very protective towards their young and have sharp teeth! In the middle of the Cletts lies the wreck of the *Darro* (locally referred to as the *Yarra Yarra*), a small steamship of 325 tons that ran aground on 18 July, 1901, carrying a cargo of coal. Depth around the boiler is 6 to 8m but a little deeper on the outside of the Cletts.

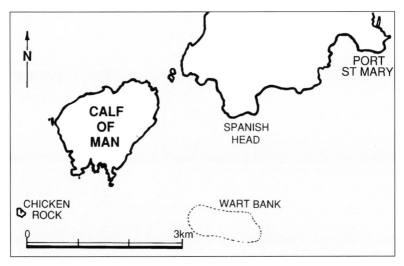

Wart Bank (site **35**)

The boiler is quite small (3m in diameter and 5m long) and exposed at LW. Most of the wreckage is north of the boiler, shallow and covered in kelp.

WHAT TO LOOK FOR: The strong currents allow filter feeders such as hydroids to grow in abundance. Also many wrasse and clean healthy kelp forest. Numerous seals.

OTHER INFORMATION: Strong current runs through the shallow water around the Cletts. Anchor downstream and swim along the bottom – rocks and the boiler provides some shelter. Best dived around slack and on neaps. Slack approximately 2hrs before LW to LW. Seals swimming happily are no indication of slack water!

35 Wart Bank

Position – 54 02 30N; 004 45 90W. *Type of Dive* – Drift. *Level of Dive* – Sports Diver/Dive Leader. *Access* – Boat Dive (launch Port Erin or Port St Mary). *Max Depth* – 40m.

DESCRIPTION: A series of sand dunes that are constantly moving due to the strong offshore currents. Although the depth off the Wart Bank is up to 40m, the range on the Bank is around 10 to 30m. The dunes run parallel in an east–west direction, with peaks 10 to 20m apart in a "saw-tooth" profile: steep on one side and gentle on the other.

WHAT TO LOOK FOR: Many shellfish and crabs, and large shoals of fish such as whiting and sand eels.

OTHER INFORMATION: Best dived $2^{1}/_{2}$ to $1^{1}/_{2}$hrs before HW and 3 to 4hrs after HW. Watch out for standing waves

Walls of living colour on Burroo Rock

THE SOUTH

This area covers dives from the Calf Sound to Fort Island, at the north-east end of Langness.

36 Carrick Nay to Burroo Ned

Position – SC 174 666 to 175 664. *Type of Dive* – Scenic. *Level of Dive* – Novice Diver. *Access* – Shore Dive (park in the Sound Café car park and follow the path south, down the steps into the gully). *Max Depth* – 14m.

DESCRIPTION: Follow the intersection between the cliffs and boulder sea bed at 10m eastwards to the Burroo Ned cliff. Safe and easy shore dive.

WHAT TO LOOK FOR: Dense kelp communities; numerous fish and crabs.

OTHER INFORMATION: There is no current, provided you do not go outside the bay or beyond Burroo Ned headland. Best to dive before HW to ensure slack water and easy access. Pleasant shore dive made even better by the close proximity of the café! *Site map:* page 78.

37 Creg y Jaghee

Position – SC 180 658 to 179 663. *Type of Dive* – Scenic/Drift. *Level of Dive* – Sports Diver. *Access* – Boat Dive (launch Port St Mary). *Max Depth* – 22m.

DESCRIPTION: During strong NE winds the high cliffs provide a lot of shelter. Drop in on the Calf Sound side close to Spanish Head and swim north. Very scenic dive.

WHAT TO LOOK FOR: Ling, pollack and wrasse, as well as a multitude of encrusting animals on the very large rock slabs.

Opposite: Steps at Cabby Ghaw, with Burroo Ned and Spanish Head in the background

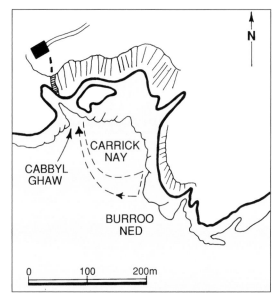

Carrick Nay to Burroo Ned (site **36**)

OTHER INFORMATION: Very little current will be encountered close inshore between Creg y Jaghee and Baie ny Briechyn if dived on the ebb. Flood tide is strong and southerly, towards Spanish Head.

38 Spanish Head to Black Head

Position – SC 181 657 to 187 657. *Type of Dive* – Scenic/Drift. *Level of Dive* – Sports Diver. *Access* – Boat Dive (launch Port St Mary). *Max Depth* – 25m.

DESCRIPTION: Huge, room-sized rocks covered with marine life make this a superb dive. Steep boulder slope drops to a flat sandy bottom with brittle-star beds interspersed with rocky outcrops.

WHAT TO LOOK FOR: Large pollack. Encrusting marine life on the rocks.

OTHER INFORMATION: Standing waves and very strong currents are encountered during maximum flood and ebb, particularly on spring tides. Slack water is from 2¹/₂ to 1¹/₂hrs before HW and 3 to 4hrs after HW. Spanish Head is so named because it is reputed that two ships of the Spanish Armada were lost here in 1588 – no wreckage has yet been found!

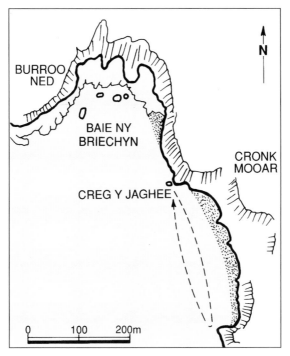

Creg y Jaghee (site **37**)

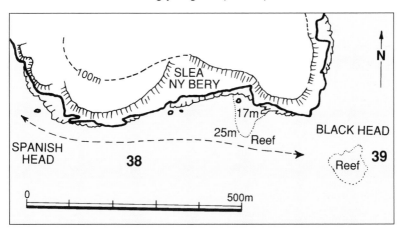

Spanish Head to Black Head – numbers in sea indicate
approximate depths at low water

39 Black Head

Position – SC 187 657. *Type of Dive* – Drift. *Level of Dive* – Sports Diver. *Access* – Boat Dive (launch Port St Mary). *Max Depth* – 25m.

DESCRIPTION: Steep slope of massive rocks and slabs leading down to a sandy sea bed. There is a rocky reef rising 6m above the bottom. Awe-inspiring dive due to the huge scale of everything.

WHAT TO LOOK FOR: Large numbers of fish such as pollack, saithe, wrasse and plaice. Plumose anemones, dead man's fingers and hydroids cover the huge rocks and reef.

OTHER INFORMATION: Currents are very strong, particularly on the ebb tide, and "pour" around Black Head. Slack tides similar to Calf Sound (site **22**): 2¹/₂ to 1¹/₂hrs before HW and 3 to 4hrs after HW. *Site map:* page 79.

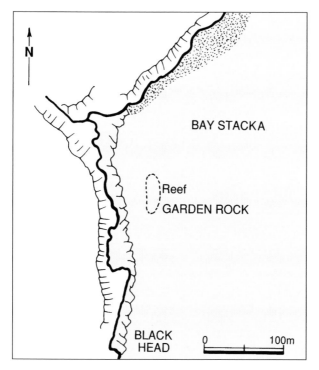

Bay Stacka (site **40**)

Sugarloaf Stack – view from the Chasms

40 Bay Stacka

Position – SC 189 661. *Type of Dive* – Scenic. *Level of Dive* – Novice Diver. *Access* – Boat Dive (launch Port St Mary). *Max Depth* – 18m.

DESCRIPTION: During strong SW to W winds, shelter can be found close to the cliffs on the west side of Bay Stacka. Close to the corner is an underwater rock rising 6m to within 8m of the surface. The east side of the rock descends steeply to a sandy bottom.

WHAT TO LOOK FOR: Wrasse, pollack and plaice. Burrowing anemones and mason worms on the undredged and thus undisturbed sand.

OTHER INFORMATION: Current sweeps around the bay and rock although it is manageable. Current increases towards Black Head. Slack water is $2^1/_2$ to $1^1/_2$hrs before HW and 3 to 4hrs after HW. A good dive if all other sites are "blown out"!

41 Sugarloaf Caves

Position – SC 195 663. *Type of Dive* – Scenic. *Level of Dive* – Novice Diver. *Access* – Boat Dive (launch Port St Mary). *Max Depth* – 16m.

DESCRIPTION: Superb cave dive and safe, as only the "V" cave is a "no-clear-surface dive" – and that does not go too far in. Fairy Hall and the Cave of the Birds have a clear surface throughout, except for the very end of the Cave of the Birds. The caves are undercut under water and "bell out", becoming quite large. Do not take an SMB as it will get caught on the sloping wall of the east end of the Fairy Hall.

WHAT TO LOOK FOR: For a photographer or marine biologist, the cave walls are fantastic, covered in encrusting animals such as gooseberry sea squirts, star sea squirts, *Morchellium, Aplidium*, oaten pipes hydroids, beadlet and *Actinothoë* anemones, and numerous elephant's ear sponges.

OTHER INFORMATION: A slight current flows through Fairy Hall (maximum 1kn), which can be disconcerting for the inexperienced if swimming against it. Site best dived around HW or with the tide ebbing (slack water is $2^1/_2$ to $1^1/_2$hrs before HW and 3 to 4hrs after HW) and even better to dive in the morning as the sun streams into the cave. During the early summer, hundreds of guillemots and kittewakes nest around the cliffs and Sugarloaf itself. It is an offence to disturb them. Do not make any sudden noises such as engine revving. If you are quiet, you will be rewarded by the wonderful sight of hundreds of birds – close up! *Site map:* page 84.

Above: Diver in Sugarloaf Caves. *Opposite:* Sugarloaf Stack

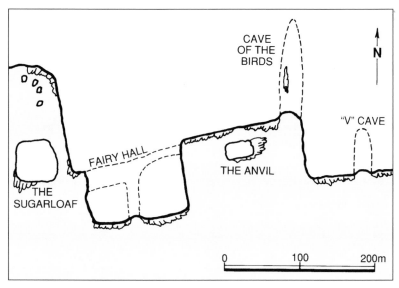

Sugarloaf Caves (site **41**)

42 Kione y Ghoggan and Traie Vane

Position – SC 199 664 to 203 668. *Type of Dive* – Scenic/Drift. *Level of Dive* – Sports Diver. *Access* – Boat Dive (launch Port St Mary). *Max Depth* – 20m.

DESCRIPTION: Sheltered from SW to N winds, the area from Kione y Ghoggan to Traie Vane makes an ideal rough weather dive. The cliffs drop down onto large rocky outcrops and ledges. There is also a small cave under Kione y Ghoggan.

WHAT TO LOOK FOR: Various fish and the usual kelp communities.

OTHER INFORMATION: Negligible currents except towards Kione y Ghoggan on an ebb tide.

43 Perwick Bay and Shag Rock

Position – SC 204 670 to 206 669. *Type of Dive* – Scenic. *Level of Dive* – Novice Diver. *Access* – Boat Dive (launch Port St Mary). *Max Depth* – 20m.

84

DESCRIPTION: Perwick Bay offers shelter from N and W winds. Dense kelp in the shallow areas leads onto a sandy sea bed in the middle of the bay. Shag rock is quite shallow (maximum 8m) but nevertheless interesting for the novice diver.

WHAT TO LOOK FOR: Fish, mainly wrasse, among the rocks and kelp and flatfish on the sand.

OTHER INFORMATION: Negligible current within the bay.

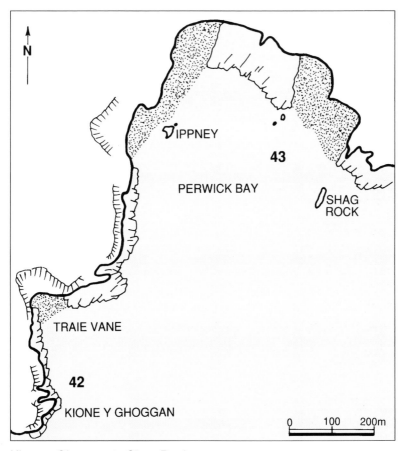

Kione y Ghoggan to Shag Rock

Aerial view of Port St Mary

44 Port St Mary Ledges and Kallow Point

Position – SC 669 211. *Type of Dive* – Scenic/Drift. *Level of Dive* –
Novice Diver/Sports Diver. *Access* – Boat Dive (launch Port St Mary).
Max Depth – 25m.

DESCRIPTION: Flat areas of bedrock and sand extending out into the bay.
Can be drift-dived in either direction as the current runs parallel to the
shore. Best to pick your own depth. Most enjoyable at around 20m, below
the kelp forest.

WHAT TO LOOK FOR: Bedrock covered in dead man's fingers and plumose
anemones; numerous gravel/stony areas. Abundant scallops and brittlestars
further offshore.

OTHER INFORMATION: Tide runs from Langness to the Sound after HW and
from the Sound to Langness before HW. About 2kn 2hrs after HW. Not
advisable to dive without boat cover.

45 The Carrick

Position – SC 227 674. *Type of Dive* – Scenic. *Level of Dive* – Novice
Diver. *Access* – Boat Dive (launch Port St Mary). *Max Depth* – 18m.

DESCRIPTION: A rock formation in the centre of Bay ny Carrickey marked with a large beacon. The rock drops in a series of wide steps down to a sand/gravel bottom. It is covered with a dense kelp forest down to about 10m. There is a very interesting wall (8 to 14m) covered in sponges and anemones on the south-east side of the Carrick – locate it with an echo sounder!

WHAT TO LOOK FOR: Gobies and blennies as well as the usual communities associated with a kelp forest. Below the kelp; wrasse, dogfish, anemones and sponges.

OTHER INFORMATION: Very little current – only up to 1kn on spring tides. Exposed to any S wind, which causes swell. *Site map:* page 88.

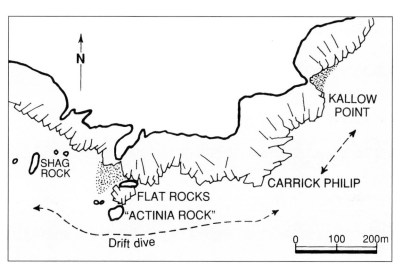

Port St Mary Ledges and Kallow Point (site **44**)

46 Poyll Vaaish

Position – SC 245 665. *Type of Dive* – Scenic/Drift. *Level of Dive* – Sports Diver. *Access* – Boat Dive (launch Port St Mary or Castletown). *Max Depth* – 20m.

DESCRIPTION: Excellent drift dive from the east side of Bay ny Carrickey, opposite the Carrick Rock around to Scarlett Point. This site can be dived on the flood or ebb tide.

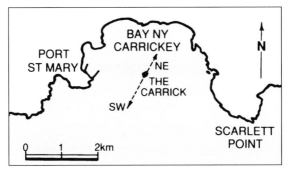

The Carrick (site **45**)

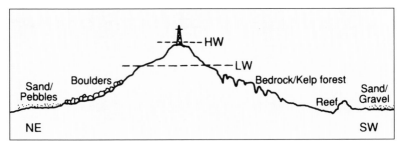

North-east to south-west transect of The Carrick (site **45**)

WHAT TO LOOK FOR: Just south of Poyll Vaaish (SC 246 668) many pieces of pottery and rifle flints are washed up onto the lower shoreline. A wreck must exist somewhere in this area.

OTHER INFORMATION: Strong current in either direction during full flood or ebb. Best dived on or around slack (1hr before HW and around LW).

47 Basalt Wall

Position – SC 255 662. *Type of Dive* – Scenic. *Level of Dive* – Novice Diver. *Access* – Boat Dive (launch Port St Mary or Castletown). *Max Depth* – 18m.

DESCRIPTION: This wall was formed by one side of a basalt dyke running west from the volcanic core of Scarlett Stack. Lying adjacent to the shore line is a vertical wall 10m high and 300m long. Numerous stacks and gullies make this a very unusual dive. About 20m further out lie a series of slate ledges.

WHAT TO LOOK FOR: Sea squirts in the narrow gullies and many varieties of fish.

OTHER INFORMATION: Best dived around HW and in early summer – before it gets too weedy! Very sheltered from N winds. There is a nature trail along the coastal footpath and a small visitors' centre at Scarlett (open during the summer, Thursday to Sunday, 2 to 5pm). *Site map:* page 90.

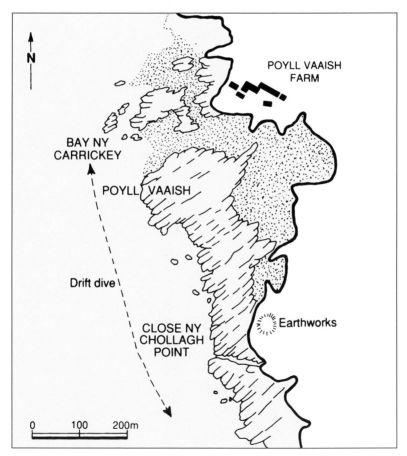

Poyll Vaaish (site **46**)

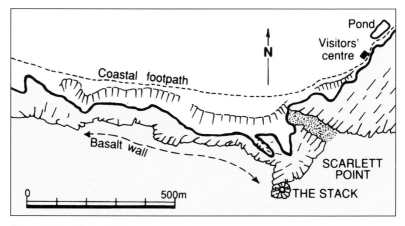

Basalt Wall (site **47**)

48 Castletown Bell Buoy

Position – SC 266 663. *Type of Dive* – Scenic/Drift. *Level of Dive* – Sports Diver. *Access* – Boat Dive (launch Port St Mary or Castletown). *Max Depth* – 20m.

DESCRIPTION: Floating in the middle of Castletown Bay, the Bell Buoy marks the outer edge of a shallow reef lying to the west of the buoy. An interesting series of slate ledges and walls run NE to SW on the Langness side of the buoy.

WHAT TO LOOK FOR: A large variety of fish including ling can be found on the ledges. Take care as there is always a lot of lost fishing gear lying around here and all around Castletown Bay.

OTHER INFORMATION: By the buoy, the current is not very strong, although it rapidly picks up further out between Langness Point and Scarlett.

The Langness peninsula The diving around Langness is exhilarating, with similar quality to the dives around the Calf of Man. Inevitably, tides are complex, localised and very strong. It is best to launch at Port St Mary (all states of the tide). Castletown or Derbyhaven can be used at around HW – though HW is not the best time to dive due to the strong currents.

The treacherous tidal currents around this exposed peninsula with its jagged, near-vertical slate rocks, combine to make this a veritable ships'

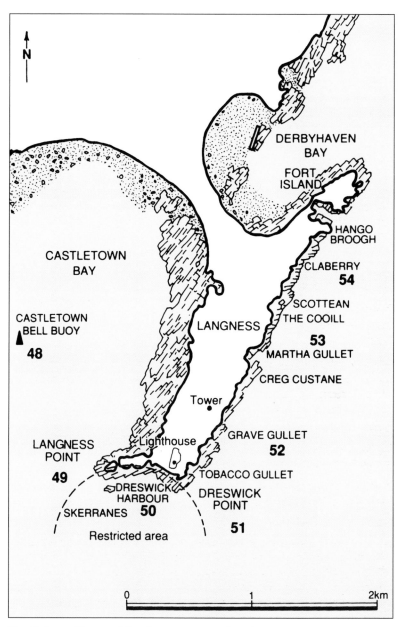

Castletown Bay and the Langness peninsula

graveyard. Over fifty ships are known to have perished around here including, in modern times, a few yachts plus the capsizing of a visiting dive boat!

At certain states of the tide, even on a calm day, standing waves form off Fort Island, Dreswick Point on the flood and the Skerranes on the ebb. The tide at Dreswick Point runs west like a raging river towards the Calf on Man and is not the place to be, even in a large boat. On the flood, the tide forms an anti-clockwise circular current on the outside of Langness. This creates a run inshore from Fort Island to Dreswick Point that is continuous for 8 out of 12 hours, only reversing at the latter part of the ebb.

Situated either side of the Langness peninsula, Castletown Bay and Derbyhaven Bay have independent circular tides. The tide in Castletown Bay is quite complex, contra-rotating for several hours.

Langness, with Fort Island in the foreground

Drift dives are excellent provided care is taken when planning, with a large SMB and reliable boat cover. Remember that it is almost impossible to pick up a diver who has drifted into an area of standing waves.

The best known ship to have been wrecked on Langness was HMS *Racehorse*, a naval brig-of-war that ended up on rocks off Langness Point on 14 December, 1822.

The 18-gun *Racehorse* was under the command of Captain William Suckling, a cousin of Lord Nelson. She was sailing to Douglas in order to accompany the partially repaired but still crippled Admiralty cutter *Vigilant* back to England. *Vigilant* had been badly damaged on rocks in Douglas Bay earlier that year. The *Racehorse* never reached Douglas. Her navigator mistook the lights at Scarlett House, Castletown for Douglas Harbour and in the late afternoon hit the Skerranes. The bottom of the ship was ripped open by the Skerranes and most of the ballast and stores sank among the rocks and gullies. Later, the main superstructure drifted to its final resting position off Dreswick Point.

Tribute was paid to the efforts of local people to save the crew of nearly 100 men. The final death toll was six crew plus three local people drowned when their boat capsized. Being a Admiralty ship, exceedingly detailed records were kept of the subsequent inquiry into the loss of the *Racehorse* and the men.

After the initial salvage attempts the only recorded effort to find anything left from the *Racehorse* was in 1844. On 29 June, the *Manx Sun* reported:

" The *Argyle of Jersey*, a smack belonging to a company in the West of England, came to Castletown Bay on Thursday last for the purpose of taking up the brass guns and other parts of the wreck of the sloop-of-war *Racehorse*, lost on Langness Point about 21 years ago. She has a diver on board with a complete apparatus, who can stay four hours at once underwater and walk miles, followed by a small boat that attends to pump air down to him ... "

The diver managed to salvage 30 tons of pig iron, a quantity of copper and a large anchor and chain.

With so many other vessels having been wrecked on Langness, HMS *Racehorse* faded from memory until 1968 when Brian King and a group of divers hunted for the wreck. It was found eventually by the Corlett brothers of Laxey. There was no difficulty in identifying items found from the brig as the Admiralty stamped every single article on board with a broad arrow mark.

The Isle of Man Sub-Aqua Club were anxious that this interesting piece of history should not be cannibalised like other wrecks, and purchased the

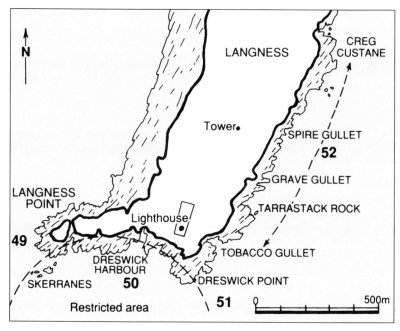

Langness – Langness Point to Creg Custane

now scattered remains from the Admiralty in 1969. The Isle of Man Department of Ports and Properties then made a restriction order covering the area from Langness Point and the Skerranes to Dreswick Point. A number of interesting items of historical (rather than commercial) value have been recovered over the years. These are now preserved in the Manx Museum and are displayed occasionally. The restriction order will be lifted when the work is complete.

Sites **49**, **50** and **51** are, at the time of writing, within the restricted area: while this remains in operation they should not be dived. Information on these sites has been included for future reference, as they are excellent dives!

49 Langness Point [in restricted area]

Position – SC 276 653 . *Type of Dive* – Scenic/Drift/Wreck. *Level of Dive* – Sports Diver/Dive Leader. *Access* – Boat Dive (launch Port St Mary). *Max Depth* – 25m or more.

DESCRIPTION: Very exposed, high energy site of jagged rocks and gullies. It may be dived only in very calm conditions and for only 2hrs in every 12. It is very easy to get lost and disorientated in the gullies.

WHAT TO LOOK FOR: Below the kelp line, all the rocks are covered with masses of the oaten pipes hydroid and patches of jewel anemones. Wide variety of fish and many seals that haul out on the rocks around LW.

OTHER INFORMATION: Diving not permitted at the time of writing. There is no wreckage visible, except for a few ballast pigs. The wreck is owned by the Isle of Man Sub-Aqua Club.

50 Dreswick Harbour (Langness Gully) [in restricted area]

Position – SC 282 653. *Type of Dive* – Scenic. *Level of Dive* – Novice Diver/Sports Diver. *Access* – Shore Dive (park at the lighthouse *only* with prior permission from the lighthouse keeper on 01624 822530). *Max Depth* – 17m.

DESCRIPTION: A very safe and sheltered dive when the wind is in the northerly quarter. Excellent novice dive within the confines of the steep-sided gully. A more advanced dive can be obtained by moving outside the gully – but keeping inshore. Several caves to be explored. A small gully to the west is full of Welsh slates – evidence of an old wreck.

Dreswick Harbour

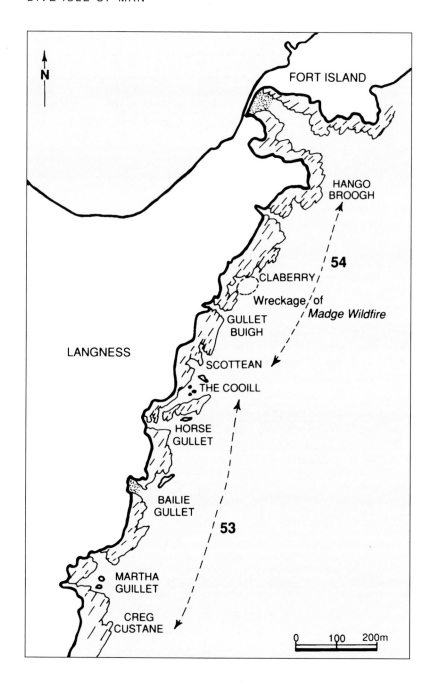

WHAT TO LOOK FOR: Seals visit the gully frequently. Rich community of algae in the shallows. Wrasse, gobies, scorpion fish and sea squirts.

OTHER INFORMATION: Diving not permitted at the time of writing. The wreck is owned by the Isle of Man Sub-Aqua Club. The land belongs to the Palace Hotel Group, owners of the golf course; cars are not allowed access beyond the car park except on lighthouse business.

51 Dreswick Point [in restricted area]

Position – SC 284 651. *Type of Dive* – Drift/Wreck. *Level of Dive* – Dive Leader. *Access* – Boat Dive (launch Port St Mary or Castletown). *Max Depth* – 26m.

DESCRIPTION: The very strong currents and jagged pinnacles of rock have always been a danger to shipping. The SS *Countess of Eglinton,* a three-masted steamer built in 1865 for the Belfast to Ardrossan route was wrecked here on 14 July, 1871. At the time she was operating between Silloth and Dublin, stopping off at Douglas. Nothing appears to remain of the wreck.

WHAT TO LOOK FOR: Shoals of pollack, wrasse and many other fish. Below the kelp, the rocks are covered with dense mats of oaten pipes hydroid and jewel anemones. Approximately 400m south of Dreswick Point lie the remains of a large paddle wheel.

OTHER INFORMATION: Diving not permitted at the time of writing. The wreck is owned by the Isle of Man Sub-Aqua Club. Care must be taken due to the very strong currents. In separate incidents, two local divers were swept away by the strong tides in this area. The first was picked up several hours later by the RNLI who, due to intimate tidal knowledge, were able to locate the diver. In the second case, the diver eventually got ashore at Port St Mary, nearly five miles away! *Site map:* page 94.

52 Tobacco Gullet to Creg Custane

Position – SC 285 652 to 289 660. *Type of Dive* – Scenic/Drift. *Level of Dive* – Sports Diver. *Access* – Boat Dive (launch Port St Mary or Castletown). *Max Depth* – 22m.

DESCRIPTION: This dive covers the following sites: Tobacco Gullet, Tarrastack Rock, Grave Gullet, Spire Gullet, The Goayr and Creg Custane.

Opposite: Langness – Creg Custane to Fort Island

An area of gullies and rock outcrops. Either drift dive in 20 to 22m over a mainly rocky sea bed or explore the deeply indented gullies.

WHAT TO LOOK FOR: Wreckage can be found in several of the gullies. By Tarrastack Rock, there is a superb, deep gully, with an overhanging cliff on the south side. This is covered in gooseberry sea squirts.

OTHER INFORMATION: Beware of pot lines when drift diving. Tide runs SE for 4hrs either side of HW. There can be an area of confused sea when the tide changes, making diver recovery difficult. *Site map:* page 94.

53 Martha Gullet to The Cooill

Position – SC 289 661 to 292 666. *Type of Dive* – Scenic/Drift. *Level of Dive* – Sports Diver. *Access* – Boat Dive (launch Port St Mary or Castletown). *Max Depth* – 22m.

The "Provider Stone", Langness

The *Madge Wildfire* on the rocks at Claberry, March 1941 (site **54**)

DESCRIPTION: This dive covers the following sites: Martha Gullet, Bailie Gullet, Horse Gullet and The Cooill. Martha and Horse Gullet are fairly large and provide considerable shelter.

WHAT TO LOOK FOR: Horse Gullet is next to the 17th tee and is locally referred to as "Golf Ball Alley" due to an impressively large number of lost golf balls!

OTHER INFORMATION: Beware of pot lines when drift diving. Tide runs SE for 4 hours either side of HW. There can be an area of confused sea when the tide changes, making diver recovery difficult. *Site map:* page 96.

54 Scottean to Hango Broogh

Position – SC 292 667 to 296 672. *Type of Dive* – Scenic/Drift/Wreck. *Level of Dive* – Sports Diver. *Access* – Boat Dive (launch Port St Mary or Castletown). *Max Depth* – 22m.

DESCRIPTION: This dive covers the following sites: Scottean, Gullet Buigh, Claberry, Gullet Creagh Moainee and Hango Broogh. Exciting drift dive or explore the various gullies. The SS *Madge Wildfire* (formally *Jerfalcon*), 140 feet long and 348 tons, built in 1905, was wrecked at Claberry on 1 March, 1941. A typical example of a two-hold general

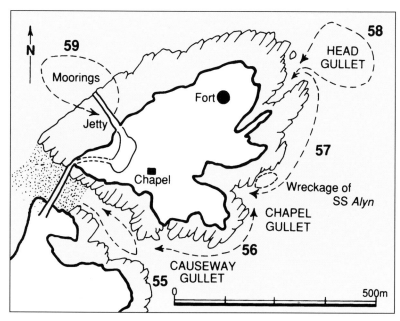

Fort Island

coaster very common around the British Isles, she was carrying a cargo of flour and soap, which resulted in a situation akin to *Whisky Galore*, as soap was rationed during the war and thus was exceedingly treasured! The ship was subsequently broken up by a salvage contractor.

WHAT TO LOOK FOR: There is a concrete plinth (used for anchoring salvage tackle) set among the rocks on the shore, which is a good indicator of where the *Madge Wildfire* was wrecked. At low tide, the engine cylinder block is just visible.

OTHER INFORMATION: Beware of pot lines when drift diving. Tide runs SE towards Dreswick for 4 hours either side of HW. *Site map:* page 96.

Fort Island   St Michael's Isle – locally known as Fort Island – is a rocky little island connected to the Langness peninsula by a short causeway. Five dives are described, but there are many other sites that can be explored. The outside of the island is swept by strong currents at all times except around LW. Fort Island is very interesting for the marine biologist or underwater photographer as it possesses high and low energy sites giving a wide diversity of habitats and a correspondingly high variety of life. There are several old anchors around Fort Island. *Please do not remove.*

The parking area is immediately after the causeway, providing access to the jetty. Random parking is no longer permitted by Manx Heritage owing to the damage caused by vehicles to the turf. Allow plenty of time to carry equipment as it is a long hike to dive sites **57** and **58**.

55 Causeway Gullet

Position – SC 295 672. *Type of Dive* – Scenic. *Level of Dive* – Novice Diver. *Access* – Shore Dive. *Max Depth* – 10m.

DESCRIPTION: Ideal novice site, being shallow (10m) and sheltered from N and W winds. Follow the bottom of the rock line around the gullet, taking care not to go outside and into the current.

WHAT TO LOOK FOR: The only eel grass bed (*Zostera*) around the Isle of Man is found here and is currently being studied – *please do not disturb.* There is plenty of life in the rock gullies with burrowing anemones in sand and shingle in the centre of the gullet.

OTHER INFORMATION: Dive to HW only – otherwise insufficient depth and tricky access – but remember that the current is running very strongly just outside the gullet towards Dreswick Point.

56 Causeway Gullet to Chapel Gullet

Position – SC 297 672. *Type of Dive* – Scenic. *Level of Dive* – Sports Diver. *Access* – Shore Dive or Boat Dive (launch Port St Mary or Castletown). *Max Depth* – 22m.

DESCRIPTION: Cliffs and gullies. The rocks and gullies meet the sand at 15m.

WHAT TO LOOK FOR: Huge variety of encrusting animals, especially anemones, sponges and hydroids. Patches of mearle among the shingle.

OTHER INFORMATION: Slack is between 1hr before LW and 1/2hr after LW. Unless you have boat cover, *do not* try to dive at any time other than at slack water.

57 Chapel Gullet to Head Gullet

Position – SC 298 674. *Type of Dive* – Scenic/Wreck. *Level of Dive* –
Sports Diver. *Access* – Shore Dive or Boat Dive (launch Port St Mary or
Castletown). *Max Depth* – 20m.

DESCRIPTION: Not a novice dive! Can be done as a shore dive with local
knowledge but care must be taken in order to exit at Head Gullet as there
are no other easy exit points this side of Fort Island. Take care! There is a
small amount of wreckage 30m N of Chapel Gullet in about 6m (LW).
This is all that remains of the *Alyn*, a 350-ton, 142ft steam ship that was
wrecked here 17 March, 1940. She was on overnight passage from Preston
to Belfast with a cargo of coal. The Langness Peninsula lighthouse was
inoperative during the war years and in addition, night visibility was poor.
Both lifeboats and a life-raft were lowered and of the nine crew, two lost
their lives from the raft. Small pieces of coal from her cargo can still be
seen lying on top of shingle around Fort Island.

WHAT TO LOOK FOR: The very strong currents at this site ensure an
incredible variety of anemones, sponges, crustaceans and hydroids.

OTHER INFORMATION: *Do not* try to dive this site at any time other than at
slack water. When shore diving, keep to a depth range of 12 to 14m, stay
close inshore and do not surface offshore. Many divers have got into
difficulties here. Slack is between 1hr before LW and ¹/₂hr after LW. *Site
map:* page 100.

58 Head Gullet

Positioh – SC 298 675. *Type of Dive* – Scenic. *Level of Dive* – Sports
Diver. *Access* – Shore Dive or Boat Dive (launch Port St Mary or
Castletown). *Max Depth* – 22m.

DESCRIPTION: Dive along the gullet, explore the entrance and the adjacent
area south but make sure you can navigate back! Stick to the rock line in
15m. Again, not a novice dive – local knowledge advisable.

WHAT TO LOOK FOR: Huge variety of marine life – as diverse as any site on
the Calf.

OTHER INFORMATION: Slack is between 1hr before LW to ¹/₂hr after LW. Do
not try to dive at any other time than at slack water. When shore diving,
keep to a depth range of 12 to 14m, stay close inshore and do not surface
offshore, otherwise the current will take you towards Santon Head. *Site
map:* page 100.

The SS *Alyn*, wrecked in March 1940 (site **57**)

59 Moorings

Position – SC 294 674. *Type of Dive* – Scenic. *Level of Dive* – Novice Diver/Sports Diver. *Access* – Shore Dive (jetty). *Max Depth* – 15m.

DESCRIPTION: Access via the small jetty on the NW side of Fort Island. A fairly sheltered site, best dived around HW, when the maximum depth is 15m. Can dive either around the moorings or else along the rock line. When diving the moorings remember that a compass is unreliable due to the large number of ground chains. Only a very slight current is present within Derbyhaven Bay, becoming strong towards the tip of Fort Island.

WHAT TO LOOK FOR: A dense forest of bootlace weed can be found off the end of the jetty, with burrowing anemones and flatfish further offshore.

OTHER INFORMATION: Several old anchors can be found. Be aware of boat traffic. *Site map:* page 100.

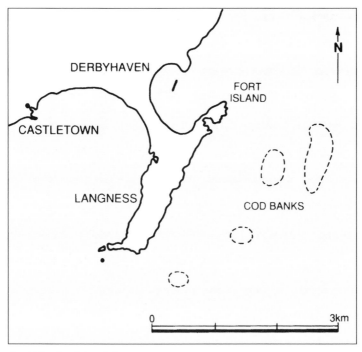

Cod Banks (site **60**)

60 Cod Banks

Position – 54 04 00N; 004 35 80W. *Type of Dive* – Drift. *Level of Dive* – Sports Diver/Dive Leader. *Access* – Boat Dive (launch Port St Mary or Castletown). *Max Depth* – 30m.

DESCRIPTION: Cod Banks lie approximately 1nm SE of Langness. Some banks consist of rocks and others are sand. They can shift due to the very strong currents.

WHAT TO LOOK FOR: Beds of cockles and mearle with the sand banks going up and down in huge in huge steps. There used to be large shoals of cod – unfortunately no longer – probably fished out. Shoals of whiting and sand eels.

OTHER INFORMATION: The current is at its weakest around 1hr before HW and 1hr before LW. Shortly after HW, the SW ebb tide starts at the Skerranes and speeds up to 5kn, 3hrs after HW, and very large standing waves. The NE flood occurs off the lighthouse and speeds up to 5kn, 3hrs before HW. Pick calm neap conditions to enjoy this unusual dive.

Opposite: Clavelina lepardiformis – lightbulb sea squirt

THE SOUTH-EAST

This area covers dives from Derbyhaven Bay to Douglas Head. Generally, the east coast is shallow (not exceeding 15m inshore). The sea bed consists of sand, gravel and rock patches. This area provides some excellent diving, being sheltered from NW winds and less frequently dived than the south.

61 Gantry Ledges

Position – SC 290 682 to 299 690. *Type of Dive* – Scenic/Drift. *Level of Dive* – Novice Diver. *Access* – Boat Dive (launch Derbyhaven). *Max Depth* – 14m.

DESCRIPTION: To the east of Ronaldsway Airport near the main runway gantry is a sunken cliff approx 200m out, parallel to the shore. It is easily located with an echo-sounder as it drops from 7m to 14m. The main ledge is up to 6m high and formed by the edge of horizontal slate beds. In places, the ledges are split by crevasses and halfway along there is a chain of small caves running back some 40m. (Cave: SC 294 684.)

WHAT TO LOOK FOR: The narrow horizontal fissures that run along this ledge provide a multitude of habitats for small creatures such as gobies, butterfish, blennies, conger eels, bloody Henry starfish and spiny squat lobsters. Snakelocks, anemones, feather duster worms and mason worms are abundant on the boulders at the base of the cliff.

OTHER INFORMATION: Although the current is slight (1kn maximum) along the ledge it becomes stronger further out into the bay. *Site map:* page 108.

62 Port Soldrick and the William Hanbury

Position – SC 308 697. *Type of Dive* – Scenic/Wreck. *Level of Dive* – Novice Diver. *Access* – Boat Dive (launch Castletown, Derbyhaven or Douglas). *Max Depth* – 15m.

Opposite: Diver with jelly fish (*Rhizostoma pulmo*).

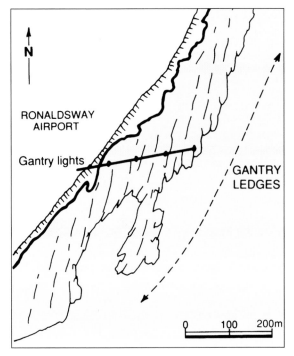

Gantry Ledges (site **61**)

DESCRIPTION: Port Soldrick (or Jackdaw Bay as it is locally known) is a small shallow bay between Port Grenaugh and Santon Gorge. The sea bed in this area tends to be shallow with an abundance of kelp. About 300m NE of Port Soldrick Bay lie the remains of the steam trawler *William Hanbury*. She ran aground on 19 January, 1942, whilst sailing from Fleetwood to the West of Scotland fishing grounds. All the crew landed safely. Little remains of the 115ft, 204-ton ship, she is very broken up but the boiler and ribs are still visible. The boiler is just outside the gully.

WHAT TO LOOK FOR: Best way to locate the wreckage is to find the rock with an "eye" in it. The wreckage is in the entrance of a small gully.

OTHER INFORMATION: No current on the wreck and very little along the coast inshore.

63 Port Grenaugh

Position – SC 316 704. *Type of Dive* – Scenic. *Level of Dive* – Novice Diver. *Access* – Shore Dive. *Max Depth* – 12m.

DESCRIPTION: A shallow and very sheltered bay-facing SE. There is no current within the bay and only a slight current outside. The visibility is generally excellent. There are rocks either side of the bay, a small reef on the west side with a sandy patch in the middle. Several telephone cables run out of the bay.

WHAT TO LOOK FOR: Many flatfish on the sand and wrasse among the rocks.

OTHER INFORMATION: Port Grenaugh is reached via the old Castletown Road. Good for walks along the scenic coastal path in either direction. *Site map:* page 110.

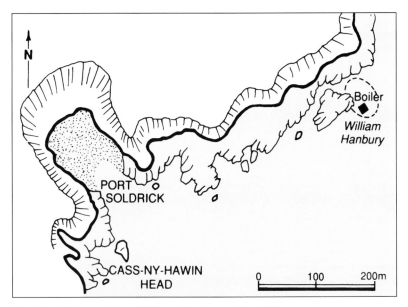

Port Soldrick and the *William Hanbury* (site **62**)

The *William Hanbury* in 1942 (site **62**)

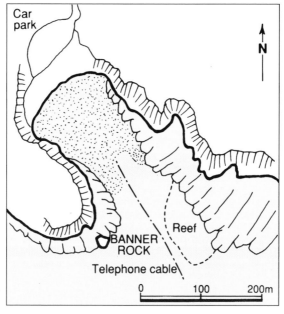

Port Grenaugh (site **63**)

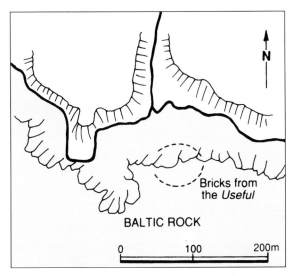

Baltic Rock (site **64**)

64 Baltic Rock

Position – SC 327 702. *Type of Dive* – Scenic/Drift. *Level of Dive* – Novice Diver/Sports Diver. *Access* – Boat Dive (launch Castletown, Derbyhaven or Douglas). *Max Depth* – 16m.

DESCRIPTION: Interesting drift dive – sea bed consisting of angular slate slabs and rocky outcrops approximately 100m offshore. Immediately east from Baltic Rock, lying in a shallow cove, bricks are to be found – the cargo of the *Useful*. She was the last of the Dee River schooners. In January 1947 she encountered heavy seas and thick fog and sailed broadside onto the jagged rocks loaded with a cargo of bricks and tiles. The crew fired distress rockets and then set fire to the galley in a bid to attract attention! There were no casualties – but the *Useful* was soon smashed to pieces.

WHAT TO LOOK FOR: Many different species of fish including dogfish, saithe, pollack and wrasse. Very large numbers of *Actinothoë* anemones and a few scallops.

OTHER INFORMATION: Current fairly strong near Santon Head but reduced inshore and towards Port Grenaugh.

111

65 Santon Head

Position – SC 334 702. *Type of Dive* – Scenic/Drift/Wreck. *Level of Dive* – Sports Diver. *Access* – Boat Dive (launch Castletown, Derbyhaven or Douglas). *Max Depth* – 25m.

DESCRIPTION: Extending from Santon Head SE for about 400m is a very interesting rock reef. It slopes on the westerly side but is steep and bisected by gullies on the easterly side. Drifting off the reef reveals another interesting area of large slate slabs. There is some wreckage on the shore next to Santon Head, the remains of the SS *Argo,* a steamer that ran aground with a cargo of iron ore and wine on 28 December, 1905.

WHAT TO LOOK FOR: The gullies on the SW side of the reef have walls covered in dead man's fingers and a good variety of other life. Fish are plentiful. The gentle slope on the NE side is not so interesting.

OTHER INFORMATION: The currents are strong on the flood (NE) and the ebb (SW). Pick times of slack water if you wish to stay on the reef. Slack

The SS *Argo* aground at Santon Head, 1905 (site **65**)

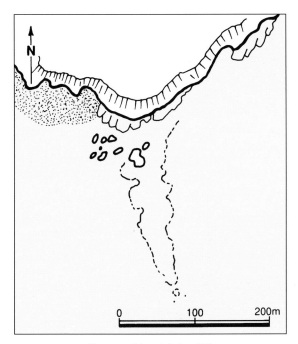

Santon Head (site **65**)

water is roughly 5hrs after HW. The reef is very easy to pick up on an echo sounder.

66 Pistol Castle

Position – SC 340 714. *Type of Dive* – Drift. *Level of Dive* – Novice Diver/Sports Diver. *Access* – Boat Dive (launch Castletown, Derbyhaven or Douglas). *Max Depth* – 15m.

DESCRIPTION: Below the sheer cliffs of this part of the coast is an area not often visited due to its distance from launch sites. Gentle drift dive down boulder slopes towards the large rocks around Santon Head. Sandy sea bed further offshore.

WHAT TO LOOK FOR: Sponges along the north face of some of the rock outcrops and dead man's fingers. Numerous fish.

OTHER INFORMATION: Relatively little current close in. *Site map:* page 114.

113

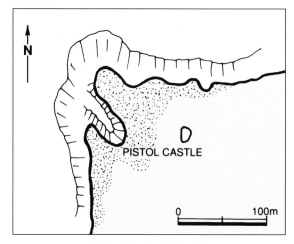

Pistol Castle (site **66**)

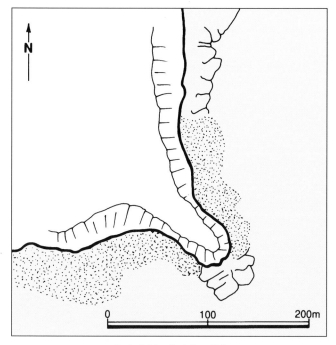

Gob Lhiack (site **67**)

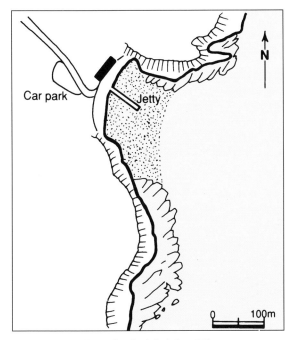

Port Soderick (site **68**)

67 Gob Lhiack

Position – SC 348 719. *Type of Dive* – Scenic/Drift. *Level of Dive* –
Novice Diver/Sports Diver. *Access* – Boat Dive (launch Castletown,
Derbyhaven or Douglas). *Max Depth* – 15m.

DESCRIPTION: A small rocky headland, Gob Lhiack is characterised by the
steep cliffs above and steep gullies below water.

WHAT TO LOOK FOR: Plenty of marine life around the cliffs and gullies.
Plaice and pollack out on the sand. Sponges on the vertical walls of the
rocky gullies.

OTHER INFORMATION: Current can run quite strongly, especially further
offshore. SMB advisable.

115

68 Port Soderick

Position – SC 347 726. *Type of Dive* – Scenic. *Level of Dive* – Novice
Diver. *Access* – Shore Dive. *Max Depth* – 14m.

DESCRIPTION: Port Soderick is a shallow sheltered SE-facing bay. A long
concrete jetty makes access to the water easy and, though shallow, this site
is particularly safe for novices as currents inshore are very slight. There
are many interesting rock outcrops towards the north of the bay. Safe to
dive at any state of tide, though currents are stronger towards the
headlands. Good drift diving offshore.

WHAT TO LOOK FOR: Port Soderick Bay was nicknamed "Barracuda Bay"
because of the number of aircraft lost during bombing practice. Engine
blocks and parts of fuselage have been found – so you never know what
will turn up!

OTHER INFORMATION: Beautiful, sheltered glen for walking; also the Marine
Drive coastal path to Douglas. There are car parks at the top (very large)
and the bottom of the steep road. There is also a bar and café at the Port
Soderick complex. *Site map:* page 115.

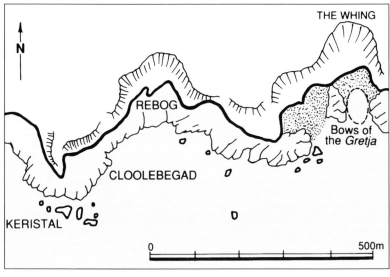

Keristal and the *Gretja* (site **69**)

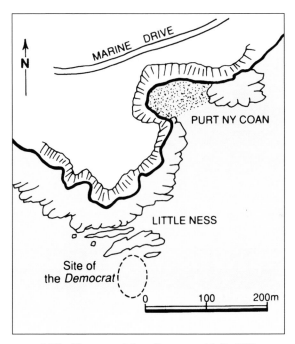

Little Ness and the *Democrat* (site **70**)

69 Keristal to Little Ness

Position – SC 352 727 to 365 727. *Type of Dive* – Drift/Wreck. *Level of Dive* – Novice Diver/Sports Diver. *Access* – Boat Dive (launch Castletown, Derbyhaven or Douglas). *Max Depth* – 16m.

DESCRIPTION: A gentle drift along the north side of Port Soderick Bay. The sea bed is highly varied with numerous large rock outcrops. In one of the small bays between Keristal and Little Ness lies the wreck of the MV *Gretja* (SC 360 732). She was a 150ft Dutch coaster with a cargo of coal that ran aground in a snow storm in the late 1960s. The bow is high up on the beach. The remains of the wreckage lie close inshore – very broken up.

WHAT TO LOOK FOR: All types of fish and shellfish. Wreckage of another Barracuda aeroplane has been seen. Large numbers of sand mason worms.

OTHER INFORMATION: Stronger currents further offshore, especially towards Little Ness.

Marine Drive – Slack Indigo and Fiddler's Green

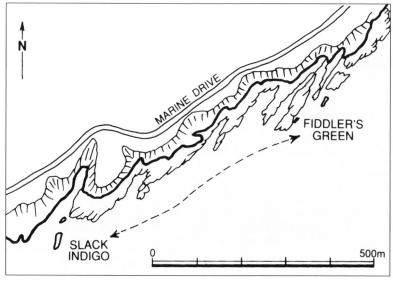

Marine Drive (site **71**)

70 Little Ness and the Democrat

Position – SC 367 728. *Type of Dive* – Wreck/Drift. *Level of Dive* – Sports Diver. *Access* – Boat Dive (launch Castletown, Derbyhaven or Douglas). *Max Depth* – 20m.

DESCRIPTION: A very interesting dive, on the rocky outcrops below the cliffs of Marine Drive. The *Democrat* was a large sailing vessel that floundered on the tip of Little Ness. Wreckage from the *Democrat* can be found in the gullies, as well as debris from one the many other ships wrecked along this coast. Drift dives off Little Ness are particularly good with boulder outcrops and brittlestar beds.

WHAT TO LOOK FOR: Wreckage of a Buccaneer aeroplane has been seen in the area off Little Ness. Plenty of marine life. Huge brittlestar beds offshore.

OTHER INFORMATION: Strong tides present. Slack at LW and 4hrs before HW. *Site map:* page 117.

71 Marine Drive

Position – SC 368 730 to 391 748. *Type of Dive* – Scenic/Drift. *Level of Dive* – Sports Diver. *Access* – Boat Dive (launch Castletown, Derbyhaven or Douglas). *Max Depth* – 20m.

DESCRIPTION: Nearly two miles of rocks and gullies to explore – good drift dive. Two exceptionally pleasant areas are Fiddler's Green and Slack Indigo, half and three quarters of a mile respectively SW from Douglas Head.

WHAT TO LOOK FOR: During the Edwardian and Victorian period pleasure boats cruised very frequently between Douglas and Port Soderick, resulting in some very interesting finds on the sea bed.

OTHER INFORMATION: Do beware of shipping near Douglas Harbour. A brisk drift dive during maximum ebb and flood (roughly mid tide), especially around Little Ness.

72 Douglas Head – the Bottle Run

Position – SC 400 750. *Type of Dive* – Drift. *Level of Dive* – Sports Diver/Dive Leader. *Access* – Boat Dive (launch Douglas). *Max Depth* – 32m.

DESCRIPTION: SE of Douglas and probably all the way to Liverpool lies a trail of debris thrown from ferries and other passenger boats over many decades. No diver should come back empty handed and many interesting objects have been found.

WHAT TO LOOK FOR: All types of bottles, plates, pottery and cutlery.

OTHER INFORMATION: Douglas harbour: diving is not in any way permitted in or around this busy commercial harbour. The new breakwater with its triangular stabit blocks may appear to be a good dive site, but it is not permitted – wave surge can also trap divers between the blocks. Care must be taken not to dive in the entrance to the harbour – be aware of ferry activities!

Douglas harbour and town

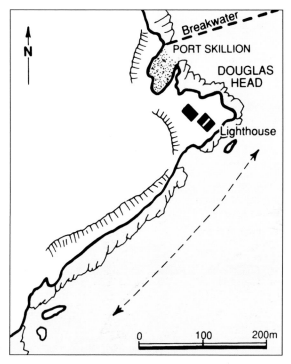

Douglas Head (site **72**)

Opposite: Calliostoma zizphinum – painted top shell

THE NORTH-EAST

This area covers dives from Douglas Bay to Ramsey. This stretch of coastline tends to be fairly shallow, particularly inshore, with a sand and gravel sea bed.

73 Mary Healey

Position = SC 413 774. Type of Dive = Scenic/Wreck. Level of Dive = Novice Diver. Access = Boat Dive (launch Douglas). Max Depth = 14m.

DESCRIPTION: The *Mary Healey* was a trawler that became wrecked during storms in the late 1940s. Plates, ribs and mast lie within the numerous gullies. Interesting area of large boulders. The boiler is visible at LW below the end house on the cliff top.

WHAT TO LOOK FOR: Take care to avoid the area of the Port Jack sewer outfall, three quarters of a mile to the west of this wreck. Moves are being made to close it, but at the time of writing this sewer is still operational.

OTHER INFORMATION: Safe to dive on any state of the tide. Cables can be seen above HW on the rocks adjacent to this wreck. *Site map: page 124.*

74 Ballina

Position = 54 09 49N; 004 14 40W. Type of Dive = Wreck. Level of Dive = Dive Leader. Access = Boat Dive (launch Douglas). Max Depth = 36m.

DESCRIPTION: Built in Barrow in 1878, the SS *Ballina* was a 341-ton steamer. On 14 January, 1882, after leaving Liverpool for her home port of Ballina, County Mayo, she sank with all hands. The wreck was discovered by Mike and John Corlett in 1967. In May 1994 the 52lb bell was returned home to the people of Ballina by Mike and Sylvia Corlett. The bell is of great significance and sentimental value to the town and will eventually be housed in a new maritime museum. The SS *Ballina* now lies 5nm east from Onchan Head and sits upright, 3 to 4m proud of the sea bed.

Opposite: The SS Cevic at Port e Vullen, June 1927

123

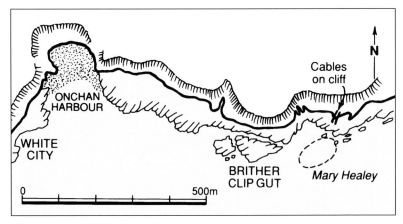

The *Mary Healey* (site **73**)

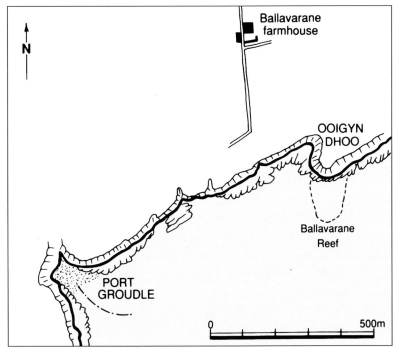

Port Groudle and Ballavarane Reef

WHAT TO LOOK FOR: In common with most wrecks, the *Ballina* is a haven for fish life; pollack, pouting and conger eels.

OTHER INFORMATION: Take care to avoid the considerable amount of fishing gear caught on the wreckage.

75 Port Groudle

Position – SC 422 782. *Type of Dive* – Scenic. *Level of Dive* – Novice Diver. *Access* – Shore Dive/Boat Dive (launch Douglas). *Max Depth* – 14m.

DESCRIPTION: Access over the steep cobbled beach. A good dive can be made by exploring around the rock line either side of the bay. The south side is steeper with several small caves. The centre of the bay consists of boulders and cobbles. Drift dive further offshore. Another pleasant dive can be had further NE along the coast, below the conspicuous Ballavarane farmhouse.

WHAT TO LOOK FOR: All types of marine life – in particular, numerous dogfish.

OTHER INFORMATION: If the sea conditions are rough, avoid the north side owing to backwash around the rocks. Road access is via the coast road from Douglas. Public car park just above beach on the left hand side. Port Groudle is also a good place for families with walks in Groudle Glen. There is a narrow-gauge railway that runs around the headland. Open at weekends – contact the Tourist Board for information.

76 Ballavarane Reef

Position – SC 428 785. *Type of Dive* – Scenic. *Level of Dive* – Sports Diver. *Access* – Boat Dive (launch Douglas). *Max Depth* – 16m.

DESCRIPTION: Reef of large rocks are boulders running seaward from the headland. Moderate to strong tide across the reef ensures plenty of marine life. The Ballavarane farmhouse is conspicuous on the hillside above this site.

WHAT TO LOOK FOR: Excellent amount of sessile life on the reef. Good variety of fish.

OTHER INFORMATION: Best dived on the ebb – running towards Douglas – when the dive can be continued along the rock line of the bay.

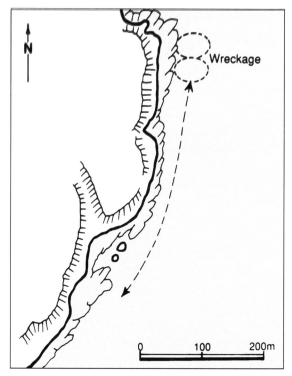

Clay Head (site **77**)

77 Clay Head

Position – SC 445 806. *Type of Dive* – Drift. *Level of Dive* – Sports Diver. *Access* – Boat Dive (launch Douglas). *Max Depth* – 15m.

DESCRIPTION: Cliff wall with numerous gullies leading to a cobble sea bed. Best dived as a drift.

WHAT TO LOOK FOR: There is the wreckage from two steamers, although little remains apart from plates and the boilers. Choose slack water in order to find the wrecks (SC 444 806).

OTHER INFORMATION: Slack is around HW and LW.

78 Bulgham Bay and the Merisia

Position – SC 458 856. *Type of Dive* – Wreck. *Level of Dive* – Novice Diver. *Access* – Boat Dive (launch Laxey or Ramsey). *Max Depth* – 12m.

DESCRIPTION: Rocks and boulders at the bottom of the cliff level out onto a cobble stone and shingle sea bed. Close inshore at the bottom of the cliffs lies the wreck of the steam trawler *Merisia*, which sank on 26 January, 1940. The crew of nine lost their lives. Large boilers, bollards, winches and chain. Wreckage lies parallel to the shore.

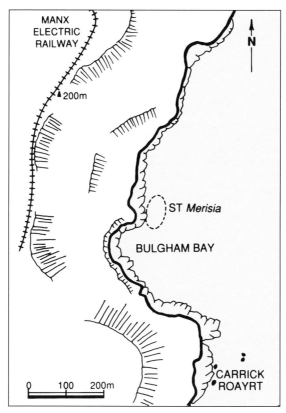

Bulgham Bay and the *Merisia* (site **78**)

127

WHAT TO LOOK FOR: Heavily overgrown by kelp. Many wrasse.

OTHER INFORMATION: Another boiler and wreckage has been found in the same area. Little or no current within the bay.

79 Port Cornaa

Position – SC 474 878. *Type of Dive* – Scenic. *Level of Dive* – Novice Diver. *Access* – Shore Dive. *Max Depth* – 12m.

DESCRIPTION: Access over a cobbled beach. Rock line on either side of the bay consists of interesting gullies, rock outcrops and ledges. Sand in middle of bay.

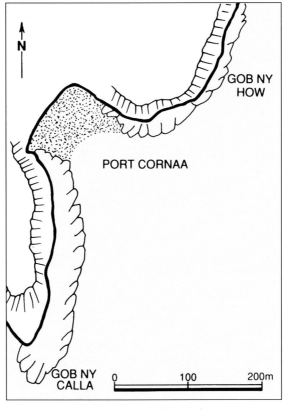

Port Cornaa (site **79**)

WHAT TO LOOK FOR: Kelp communities and many fish.

OTHER INFORMATION: Only a very slight current within the bay. Road access: take the Glen Mona road off the Laxey to Ramsey coast road. Easy parking with a good picnic area. Beautiful walks next to waterfalls in the Ballaglass Glen.

80 Robert Dee

Position – 54 15 18N; 004 19 12W. *Type of Dive* – Wreck. *Level of Dive* – Sports Diver. *Access* – Boat Dive (launch Laxey or Ramsey). *Max Depth* – 26m.

DESCRIPTION: The *Robert Dee*, a wooden trawler of 26 tons, sank after colliding with the FV *Jacob Johanes* on 18 May, 1978 . The hull is mainly broken up and scattered but the engine and winches are still present. Located half a mile offshore.

WHAT TO LOOK FOR: Large shoals of bib and pollack.

OTHER INFORMATION: Slack is 1hr either side of HW and LW.

81 Light Float

Position – 54 15 13N; 004 19 50W. *Type of Dive* – Wreck. *Level of Dive* – Sports Diver/Dive Leader. *Access* – Boat Dive (launch Laxey or Ramsey). *Max Depth* – 28m.

DESCRIPTION: Mersey Channel light float with bell tower. Sitting upright on the sea bed. Bell tower believed to be flattened during hydrographical survey in 1991.

WHAT TO LOOK FOR: The wreck is festooned with plumose anemones. Very large shoals of bib.

OTHER INFORMATION: Slack occurs approximately around HW and LW.

82 Traie ny Unaig – the Glendun and the Crown

Position – SC 479 888 (*Glendun*) and SC 481 889 (*Crown*). *Type of Dive* – Wreck. *Level of Dive* – Novice Diver. *Access* – Boat Dive (launch Laxey or Ramsey). *Max Depth* – 10m.

DESCRIPTION: The *Glendun*, a steamer from Belfast, went aground at Ballaskeig on 14 February, 1940. All the crew got off safely and rowed to

The SS *Glendun* on the rocks between Ballaskeig and Ballafayle, February 1940

Ramsey. The wreck is well broken up – the boiler is just visible at LW with most of the wreckage covered in sand or kelp. Engine, plates and ribs present. Approximately 200m north from the *Glendun* lies the *Crown*, a steam passenger ship of 266 tons that struck a small promontory of rocks just south of Traie ny Unaig on 7 November, 1906. Attempts at salvage failed in 1907. The wreck is very broken up and little remains. Both wrecks can be snorkelled.

WHAT TO LOOK FOR: Fish and crabs around the boiler and winches.

OTHER INFORMATION: Negligible current.

83 Prince Alfred

Position – SC 485 894. *Type of Dive* – Wreck. *Level of Dive* – Novice Diver. *Access* – Boat Dive (launch Laxey or Ramsey). *Max Depth* – 10m.

DESCRIPTION: In February 1869 the new 700-ton passenger and cargo steamer *Prince Alfred*, sailing from Fleetwood to Belfast, struck the rocks

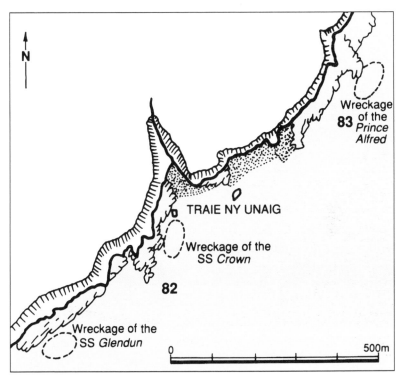

The *Glendun, Crown* and *Prince Alfred*

The SS *Crown* on rocks south of Maughold Head, November 1906

below Ballafayle in thick fog. She became a total wreck although there was no loss of passengers or crew. The wreck is very broken up and little remains – partially buried in the sand.

WHAT TO LOOK FOR: Fish and crabs.

OTHER INFORMATION: Negligible current.

84 Port Mooar

Position – SC 489 908. *Type of Dive* – Scenic. *Level of Dive* – Novice Diver. *Access* – Shore Dive. *Max Depth* – 8m.

DESCRIPTION: Shallow bay best dived or snorkelled at around HW. The east side is the better site.

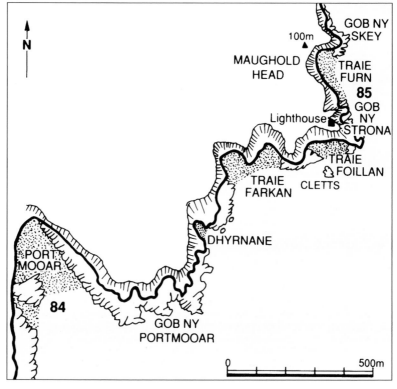

Port Mooar to Maughold Head

Maughold Head and Port Mooar from Ballajora

WHAT TO LOOK FOR: Seals regularly come into the bay and there is a lot of other marine life such as wrasse. Lots of rock pools to keep children busy.

OTHER INFORMATION: Negligible currents. The coastal footpath around Maughold Head is excellent with spectacular views around the lighthouse. A visit to Maughold Old Church with its ancient Celtic crosses is worth while.

85 Maughold Head

Position – SC 498 915. *Type of Dive* – Scenic/Drift. *Level of Dive* – Sports Diver. *Access* – Boat Dive (launch Ramsey). *Max Depth* – 14m.

DESCRIPTION: The waters around the north of the Isle of Man tend to be shallow with the sea bed consisting of sand and shingle. Maughold Head is no exception – the sea bed and rocks below the cliffs do not support the same amount of life as found in the south of the island. The cliffs below Maughold Head drop to the sandy sea bed. Further out is more interesting with rocky outcrops and reefs. The bay south of Gob ny Strona around to Port Mooar is very sheltered albeit shallow with rocky outcrops. Numerous ships have been wrecked around Maughold Head – bits of wreckage can be found.

133

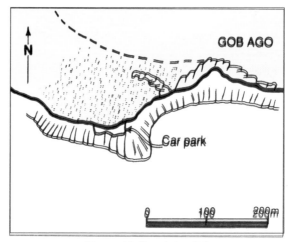

Port e Vullen (site 87)

WHAT TO LOOK FOR: There is a colony of seals living in this area and they regularly appear during dives.

OTHER INFORMATION: The strong currents around Maughold Head should be avoided, so dive around slack water (1hr before LW to 3hrs before HW).

86 Albatross

Position = 54 16 08N; 004 10 19W. *Type of Dive* = Wreck. *Level of Dive* = Sports Diver/Dive Leader. *Access* = Boat Dive (launch Laxey or Ramsey). *Max Depth* = 30m.

DESCRIPTION: The steam trawler *Albatross* was built in 1884 and was lost in a collision (five crew drowned) when run down by the *Duke of Clarence* on 6 November, 1894. The wreck now lies upright and 4m proud on a flat sea bed, approximately 5 miles east of Maughold Head.

WHAT TO LOOK FOR: Large shoals of fish. Various nets and other fishing gear present. Visibility often poor.

OTHER INFORMATION: Slack occurs approximately around HW and LW. Another reasonably large wreck lies very close to the *Albatross* – less than half a mile away. This wreck has not yet been identified.

87 Port e Vullen

Position – SC 476 927. *Type of Dive* – Scenic. *Level of Dive* – Novice Diver. *Access* – Shore Dive. *Max Depth* – 8m.

DESCRIPTION: Shallow site that can be either dived or snorkelled and is very sheltered from all S winds. Enter on the east end of the beach and dive around the "tail" of rocks 50m offshore. Scattered pieces of wreckage lying around in this area are probably remains of the trawler SS *Cevic*, which ran aground in a gale on the tip of Gob Ago on 26 June, 1927. There are also plates on the beach near Stack Mooar.

WHAT TO LOOK FOR: Seals and wrasse.

OTHER INFORMATION: Best dived around HW. No currents.

88 Fire King

Position – 54 26 08N; 004 21 72W. *Type of Dive* – Wreck. *Level of Dive* = Dive Leader/Advanced Diver. *Access* – Boat Dive (launch Ramsey). *Max Depth* – 32m (LW).

DESCRIPTION: The *Fire King* was a Liverpool Steamer built in Aberdeen in 1925. She sank on 10 December, 1939, following a collision in thick fog with the Belfast passenger steamer *Duke of Lancaster*. The *Fire King* was nearly cut in half by the bows of the larger passenger boat. The crew of twelve managed to jump from the mast rigging onto the *Duke of Lancaster* and only one man was slightly injured.

The wreck lies almost upright on a sandy bottom and is in surprisingly good condition.

WHAT TO LOOK FOR: The 200-foot, 758-ton wreck has provided a home for numerous fish such as ling and conger. She was carrying a general cargo, little of which was salvaged.

OTHER INFORMATION: It is important to dive this site on slack water as there are very strong currents around the Point of Ayre. Slack occurs 5hrs after HW but is less than one hour long even on neap tides.

THE NORTH-WEST

This area comprises the coast from the Point of Ayre to Peel Bay. The sea bed is flat, sandy and fairly shallow. There are no interesting features apart from the small Craig Rock, just north of Peel, so it is not conducive to good diving!

Several miles offshore, between Jurby Head and The Cronk, a NATO bombing range with floating targets was in use for many years until it was decommissioned in 1993. It is a no-go area for diving because of unexploded ordnance on the sea bed.

89 Peel Castle – St Patrick's Isle

Position – SC 241 845. *Type of Dive* – Scenic. *Level of Dive* – Novice Diver. *Access* – Shore Dive. *Max Depth* – 10m.

DESCRIPTION: With a maximum depth of only around 10m there is plenty of time to enjoy this shore dive. St Patrick's Isle is very exposed to all but E winds. Enter the water on Fenella Beach, close to the Castle, and follow the rock/sand boundary around the island. On the south side of the beach lies the wreck of the *St George*. Although it has now sunk into the sand, parts of the wreck are occasionally exposed after storms. The *St George* was wrecked on 7 October, 1889, and is famous for the gallant rescue of 23 people (including Captain Thoresen's baby daughter) by the crew of the Peel lifeboat. The rescue was immortalised by the poem by T.E. Brown, *The Wreck of the St. George*. In 1992, the captain's granddaughter Karen Bache Nordli launched the new Peel lifeboat, *The Ruby Clery*. In June 1994, a painting of the *St. George* was sent from Norway and is displayed in the new Peel lifeboat house.

WHAT TO LOOK FOR: Numerous dahlia anemones to be found in the many pretty gullies and caves. Mussels (SW corner); plaice and cuttlefish on the sandy sea bed. Some friendly seals frequent the harbour and the area around St Patrick's Isle.

OTHER INFORMATION: Best dived around HW in light or E winds – with other wind directions it can become very rough on the outside of the

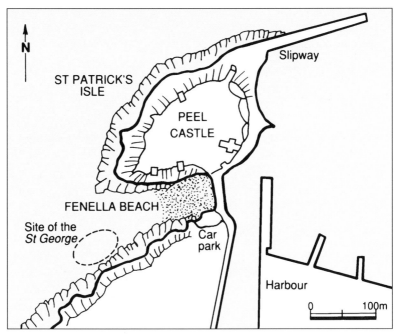

Peel Castle on St Patrick's Isle (site **89**)

Peel Castle, with Fenella beach at right

138

island, with poor visibility. When swimming around the castle ensure that enough air is left for the return journey. Diving around the breakwater is not permitted as this is a busy working harbour.

90 Sunken City (Cashtal Mooar)

Position – SC 232 833. *Type of Dive* – Scenic. *Level of Dive* – Novice Diver. *Access* – Boat Dive (Peel or Port Erin). *Max Depth* – 8 to 10m.

DESCRIPTION: Underwater rock formations give an appearance of "walls" and "rooms" with a sandy sea bed. A very unusual dive site.

WHAT TO LOOK FOR: This area is often frequented by seals. Numerous fish and dense kelp communities.

OTHER INFORMATION: Fairly strong currents near Contrary Head; negligible currents inshore around Cashtal Mooar.

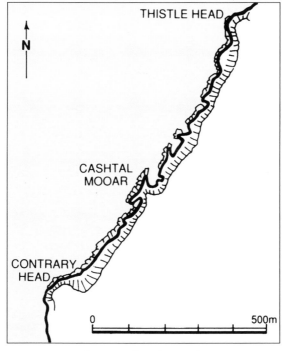

Sunken City (site **90**)

BLANK DIVE SHEET

Photocopy this form and use it to record new sites that you discover or additional information on sites described in this book. Completed forms may be kept for reference or forwarded to the authors c/o the publishers.

Dive Site: _____

Position: _____

Type of Dive: _____

Level of Dive: _____

Access: _____

Max Depth: _____

DESCRIPTION: _____

_____

_____

_____

WHAT TO LOOK FOR: _____

_____

_____

_____

OTHER INFORMATION: _____

_____

_____

_____

Name: _____

Date: _____

APPENDIX 1:
MANX COASTAL PLACE NAMES

Most of the dive sites listed in this guide have Manx place names and it is hoped that divers will make every effort to use them (and write them in their log books!). The native Manx Gaelic language is still widely spoken and taught in schools. Below is a list of some of the names used, their origin and a translation.

The key letters used for the origin of the names are:

G   Gaelic
N   Norse (via Norse invaders!)
E   English
OE Old English

Manx place name	Origin	English translation
Amulty	G	Great cliff
Ayres	N	Gravelly bank
Baie ny Briechyn	G	Bay of the breeches (shape)
Bailie Gullet	OE	Bailiff gullet
Baiy ny Ooig	G	The bay of the caves
Ballakeyll	G	Comish's farm
Ballavarane	G	Berane's farm
Bay Stacka	N/G	The bay of the stack (rock)
Bay yn Ow	G/E	The bay of the hough (cliff)
Bayr ny Skeddan	G	Herring Way
Bradda	N	Broad headland
Bulgham Bay	G	Bay of the gusty wind
Burroo	N	Fortress
Burroo Ned	N/G	Fortress of the nest
Caigher Point	G	Fortress point
Carrick Nay	G	The rock of the grave

Manx place name	*Origin*	*English translation*
Carrick Roayrt	N/G	Rock of the flood tide
Cashtal Mooar	G	Big castle
Cass-ny-Hawin	G	The foot of the river
Claberry	N	Cliff rock
Clett Aldric	N	Aldrick rock
Clett Ellby	G	Prominent rock
Creg Custane	G	Customs rock
Creg Liauyr	G	Long rock
Creg y Jaghee	G	The tithe rock
Creg Veanagh	G	Middle rock
Cronk ny Arrey Laa	G	Hill of the day-watch
Cronk y Bing	G	Shrill or melodious hill
Dreswick	N	Rock creek
Fleshwick	N	Green spot creek
Ghaw Yiarn	N/G	Iron creek
Gob Lhiack	G	Slate headland
Gob ny Calla	G	The headland of the anchorage
Gob ny Creggan	G	The headland of the rocks
Gob ny How	G/OE	The headland of the cliff
Gob ny Skey	G	The port of the wing or head
Gob ny Strona	G	The port of the stream
Gob ny Ushtey	G	The mouth of the water
Gullet Buigh	E/G	Yellow gullet
Gullet Creagh Moainee	G	Gullet of the turf stack
Kione Beg	G	Little head
Kione Meanagh	G	Middle head
Kione ny Halby	G	Headland of the promontory
Kione y Ghoggan	G	The head of the cliffs
Lhoob Doo	G	Black loop
Lhoob ny Charran	G	The loop of the white shells
Little Ness	E/N	Little promontory
Niarbyl	G	The tail

Manx place name	Origin	English translation
Ooigyn Dhoo	G	Black caves
Perwick	N	Port creek
Port Cornaa	E/N	Port of the mill-water
Port e Vullen	G	The port of the mill
Port Grenaugh	N	Green creek
Port Mooar	G	The great port
Port Soldrick	N	Sunny creek
Poyll Vaaish	G	Pool of death
Raad ny Foillan	G	Road of the gull
Rarick	N	Roe deer creek
Skerranes	N	Little rocks
Strion Vuigh	G	The yellow nose
Tarrastack Rock	G	Seaweed rock
The Carrick	N	The rocky islet
The Cletts	G	The small sea rocks
The Cooill	G	The nook
The Cronk	G	The hill
The Goayr	G	The goat
The Nay	G	The flat
The Sker	N	The rock in the sea
Traie Farkan	G	The shore of the lapwing
Traie Foillan	G	The shore of the seagull
Traie ny Unaig	N/G	The shore of the windy bay
Traie Vane	G	The white shore

APPENDIX 2:
THE DIVER'S CODE OF CONDUCT

Divers must at all times adhere to the BSAC code of conduct. It is reproduced here with the kind permission of the British Sub-Aqua Club, and has been extracted from the BSAC *Safe Diving Practices* booklet, available from BSAC Headquarters. The notes in square brackets have been added by the authors of this guide.

THE DIVER'S CODE OF CONDUCT

More and more people are taking to the water. Some for recreation; some to earn their living. This code is designed to ensure that divers do not come into conflict with other water users. It is vital that you observe it at all times.

Before leaving home

Contact the nearest British Sub-Aqua Club Branch or the dive operator local to the dive site for their advice. Seek advice from them about the local conditions and regulations.

On the beach, river bank or lakeside

1. Obtain permission, before diving in a harbour or estuary or in private water. Thank those responsible before you leave. Pay harbour dues.
2. Try to avoid overcrowding one site, consider other people on the beach.
3. Park sensibly. Avoid obstructing narrow approach roads. Keep off verges. Pay parking fees and use proper car parks.
4. Don't spread yourselves and your equipment since you may upset other people. Keep launching ramps and slipways clear.
5. Please keep the peace. Don't operate a compressor within earshot of other people – or late at night.
6. Pick up litter. Close gates. Be careful about fires. Avoid any damage to land or crops.

7. Obey special instructions such as [Manx] National Trust rules, local bye-laws and regulations about camping and caravanning [caravans are not permitted on the Isle of Man].

8. Remember divers in wetsuits are conspicuous and bad behaviour could ban us from beaches.

In and on the water

1. Mark your dive boats so that your Club can be identified easily. Unmarked boats may become suspect.

2. Ask the harbour-master or local officials where to launch your boat – and do as they say. Tell the Coastguard, or responsible person, where you are going and tell them when you are back.

3. Stay away from buoys, pots, and pot markers. Ask local fishermen where not to dive. Offer to help them recover lost gear.

4. Remember ships have not got brakes, so avoid diving in fairways or areas of heavy surface traffic and observe the "International Regulations for the Prevention of Collisions at Sea".

5. Always fly the diving flag when diving, but not when on the way to, or from, the dive site. Never leave a boat unattended.

6. Do not come in to bathing beaches under power. Use any special approach lanes. Do not disturb any seal or bird colonies with your boats. Watch your wash in crowded anchorages.

7. Whenever possible, divers should use a surface marker buoy.

On conservation

1. Never use a speargun with an aqualung. Never use a speargun in fresh water. [Spearfishing is illegal on the Isle of Man.]

2. Shellfish, such as crabs and lobsters, take several years to grow to maturity; over-collecting in an area soon depletes stocks. Only take mature fish or shellfish and then only what you need for yourself. Never sell your catch or clean it in public or on the beach. Don't display your trophies.

3. Be conservation conscious. Avoid damage to weeds and the sea bed. Do not bring up sea-fans, corals, starfish or sea urchins – in one moment you can destroy years of growth.

4. Take photographs and notes – not specimens. Shoot with a camera not a speargun – spearfishing makes fish shy of divers. Never spearfish wrasse or other inshore species since once an area is depleted of such fish, it may take a long time for them to re-colonise. [Spearfishing is illegal on the Isle of Man.]

146

On wrecks

1. Do not dive on a designated wreck site. These are indicated on Admiralty Charts and marked by buoys or warning notices on the shore nearby.
2. Do not lift anything which appears to be of historical importance.
3. It you do discover a wreck, do not talk about it. Pinpoint the site, do a rough survey and report it to the BSAC Archaeology Adviser and the Council for Nautical Archaeology [Manx Heritage on the Isle of Man] who will advise you.
4. If you do not lift anything from the wreck, it is not necessary to report your discovery to the Receiver of Wreck. If you do lift, you must report.
5. If your find is important, you may apply for it to be designated a protected site. Then you can build up a well qualified team with the right credentials and proceed with a systematic survey or excavation under licence without outside interference.

Don't Let Divers Down – Keep To The Diver's Code

BSAC BRANCHES

Diving is very popular in the Isle of Man, with six BSAC branches and a diving school (Southern Diving Lodge). For the current list of branch officers contact BSAC headquarters on 0151-357 1951. Any air station on the island can supply contact telephone numbers.

The local branches are:
   Castle Rushen Divers (branch 1287)
   Isle of Man Sub-Aqua Club (branch 76)
   Isle of Man Underwater Group (branch 996)
   Port Erin Marine Biologists' Sub-Aqua Club (branch 9177)
   Ramsey Sub-Aqua Club (branch 860)
   Southern Diving Group (branch 1465)

ACKNOWLEDGEMENTS

The authors would like to thank the following people for their time, knowledge and information:
- Mike Bates, Kevin Christian, Tony Heaton, Tim Hill, Ian Sims, Steve Taggart, Mark Whittington and Dave Woods for dive site information
- John Kermode for shipwreck details
- Bill Sleigh, George Callister and Terry Faragher for shipwreck photographs
- John C. Crellin for the translations of Manx place names
- Sara Brand for typing and checking proofs
- The Isle of Man Tourist Board for their valuable backing
- Dr Peter Astell-Burt, Shaun Cairns and the Pacini Charitable Foundation for their help and support

The Diver's Code of Conduct and the information on decompression accidents are included with the kind co-operation of the British Sub-Aqua Club.

All the colour photographs were taken by the authors, with the exception of those on page 75 (Richard Shaftoe), page 92 (Island Photographic Co Ltd) and page 138 (Manx Heritage).

The black-and-white photographs on pages 99, 103 and 110 were by W.H. Sleigh; page 38 by D.W. Kee and page 112 by W. Comery.

The original sketches for all the maps were prepared by Ben Hextall and the final artwork was drawn by Suzanne Hall.

INDEX

The bold numbers in parentheses are dive site numbers.